modern
house
three

Raul A. Barreneche

modern
house
three

Raul A. Barreneche

modern house
three

00 introduction

01 merging inside and out

02 reimagining the program

03 materials, craft and technology

04 credits/index

Never has the private house played such a large and visible role in the public consciousness. As the ultimate personal sanctuary and shelter, the home has always been important in the collective imagination. And as the most familiar and accessible building type, houses have drawn in those with an interest in architecture more easily than have museums or libraries. In the past few years, that significance has escalated as homes have come to be seen as much more than a place to live. The real estate frenzy in the United States has taken home ownership to record levels—in the US, the Census Bureau reported that at last count, 68 percent of the population owned their own homes. Like the stock market in the heyday of the 1990s, real estate is now a financial obsession for investors of every social and economic stripe. Advertisements for home financing are everywhere—on the Internet, in newspapers, and on prime-time television. And with interest rates at their lowest levels in four decades, the lure of affordable financing to buy or build a home is too great to resist.

Who can blame the public for being drawn like moths to the bright glow of the home? In magazines and on television, domesticity rules. Home improvement shows dominate the airwaves, from the BBC's "Changing Rooms" and "House Invaders" to American television's "Trading Spaces," "Sell This Home!" and dozens of others. Print media has seen an expansion from traditional shelter magazines into new domestic "lifestyle" titles, from talk show maven Oprah Winfrey's *O at Home* to the decidedly modernist *Dwell* to the offbeat, now defunct *Nest*. Such far-flung coverage of domestic pursuits reflects the public's insatiable appetite for everything related to the home. And that extrapolates into an increased awareness and appreciation of the architecture of the modern house.

The fascination with all things domestic is not limited to mass media. One of the most popular architecture shows at the Museum of Modern Art in New York in recent years was the 1999 exhibition "The Un-Private House." The show took as its premise the fact that the home is not the private hideaway it once was; rather, it is a place with a fluid relationship with the public realm caused by attitudinal shifts in family, domesticity, work habits, and digital media. Among the twenty-six projects featured in the show were houses by architects such as Herzog + de Meuron, Rem Koolhaas, and Shigeru Ban, whose provocatively deshabille Curtain Wall House in Tokyo captured the exhibition's thesis: A photogenic exterior of billowing white fabric curtains reflected many of the trends in contemporary residential architecture. There were homes with separate and shared spaces for multiple generations of the same family; a house with high-tech skins that can receive and transmit digital information; a sleek house with large installations of cutting-edge video art; and, perhaps most famously, Rem Koolhaas's revolutionary home for a wheelchair-bound client in Bordeaux, France, with a hydraulic platform that transports an entire "room" up and down through the house.

Top: The Curtain Wall House in Tokyo, designed by Shigeru Ban, plays on notions of privacy—and the concept of the curtain wall.

Above: Maison à Bordeaux, in France, designed by Rem Koolhaas, features an innovative hydraulic lift that moves space and the home's wheelchair-bound owner vertically through the house.

Like "The Un-Private House," the chapters of this book touch on themes explored by architects in the most innovative houses built around the world in recent years. The featured projects raise many of the same issues, particularly the houses in section 02 that deal with contemporary lifestyles: several generations sharing the same home, families that combine living and working under the same roof, and vacation getaways for relaxing in bare-bones or high-end style. But the houses featured in these pages deal with innovation in all its forms, in how they integrate architecture and landscape, negotiate difficult urban sites, and explore with new materials and energy-saving technologies.

Indoor-outdoor living

The houses in section 01 reveal a strong connection to the outdoors. The idea of a modern house that opens itself up to its surroundings is hardly new. Indeed, twentieth-century modernists like Mies van der Rohe, Le Corbusier, Richard Neutra, and Rudolf Schindler made the extension of interior space to the exterior a central tenet of their design philosophy. That, of course, was more easily achieved for the California modernists like Neutra and Schindler, who went so far as to install open-air sleeping decks on the roof of his house on King's

Road in West Hollywood. Schindler's home also makes a convincing case for outdoor living with an alfresco sitting room at the back, a sheltered courtyard complete with a fireplace for cool California evenings.

When climates permit, contemporary architects are following in those early modern footsteps by creating houses that fearlessly open up the indoors to the exterior. Witness the unadulterated indoor-outdoor living spaces of Steven Harris's Weiss House (page 22), Barclay & Crousse's Casa Equis (page 68), and Shigeru Ban's Picture Window House (page 80). The projects treat outside space as a fully integrated extension of the indoors, and vice-versa. Even in colder settings, architects are forging more open connections to the outdoors, although mindful of the limitations of harsh climates. Julie Snow's Koehler House on the coast of New Brunswick, Canada (page 60), and Shim-Sutcliffe's Weathering Steel House in Toronto (page 42) are successful in creating environments that offer physical and psychological shelter in winter and open spaces from which to enjoy the beauty of their landscapes in milder weather.

Architects' interest in site goes beyond dissolving external barriers; it also includes strategies for using space efficiently. Increasing land values, especially in the world's most crowded cities, have put a premium on square footage. It behooves architects in high-density locations like land-starved Japan and Holland but also in London, New York, and other cities to build homes that make more efficient use of space. By way of example, the houses in this book located in Japan reveal that with careful planning, small houses can be comfortable and functional, and they don't have to sacrifice big design ideas to fit into tiny sites. Several Tokyo projects in section 02 reveal the difficulties of squeezing the programmatic needs of busy modern families into the world's densest, most congested urban environment: houses by Toyo Ito, Kei'ichi Irie, and Kazuyo Sejima of SANAA. In her aptly named Small House (page 130), Sejima acknowledges that dividing up the miniscule floor plates with walls would make the tiny house feel even smaller. So she left the floor plans unobstructed, like mini-lofts, with a single function per floor. The plans are flexible enough so they can adapt as the family's needs change; for instance, giving the young daughter her own room when she grows older without having to reconfigure the entire house or add on to it.

Irie's C House (page 104) takes on the added burden of fitting three generations into a single home. In this case, open loft living would not have made sense; privacy for parents, grandparents, and children was key for the family in such tight quarters. Irie gave them separate and distinct bedrooms, which left little room for common living space. So he designed an ingenious, long glass table that acts as kitchen counter, dining table, and magnet for general gathering.

The Borneo Sporenburg development in Amsterdam shows the high level of design and flexibility possible at a larger scale on high-density sites. Master-planned by the Dutch firm West 8, Borneo Sporenburg comprises 2,500 dwellings on two long quays. The houses are the work of a roster of European architects, including MVRDV of Rotterdam and Barcelona's MAP Arquitectos; all of them meet master plan guidelines for diversity and uniformity. The houses are well conceived, with light wells, courtyard gardens, and even private parking, proving that comfort, high density, and design are not incompatible concepts.

The Dirty House in London by David Adjaye (page 116), like his earlier Elektra House (1999), grapples with building lofty live/work spaces in a dense urban setting—in this case the gritty wilds of East London—with a tight budget. The Dirty House cleverly screens out the city at the lower levels and opens up loft-like living spaces in the upper reaches—shielded by a parapet wall that edits out unwanted views but keeps scenic vistas of the rooftops of London. The Elektra House, designed with an even tighter budget, builds upon existing walls with new expanses of glass to create brightly lit interiors behind a solid wall of painted plywood. In these two houses, Adjaye challenges the idea that defensive urban structures must feel like closed, cramped bunkers. On the contrary: They have soaring, day-lit, double-height spaces that recall the luminous volumes of contemporary art galleries. The key to their success as functional family homes for living and working has much to do with their open, flexible character—variations on the loft typology.

Top: The Borneo Sporenburg development in Amsterdam packs high-density housing on two long piers.

Above: David Adjaye's Elektra House in London offers loft-like living on a budget.

The legacy of the loft

The loft phenomenon had its roots in the former industrial spaces reconquered by struggling artists in big cities—New York especially—in the 1970s and 1980s. Drawn by large, open floor plans, plenty of natural light, and cheap rents, artists set up their homes and studios in old cast-iron buildings once populated by warehouses and factories. Over the years, loft living, which once embodied a relaxed, bohemian quality of urban life, transformed itself from the milieu of starving artists to that of the wealthy bankers and lawyers. Converted lofts in once unsavory parts of New York, London, and other cities—even less urban Los Angeles, Seattle, and Denver—now command huge prices. As a result, artists have been squeezed out of the very phenomenon they helped create. Part of the attraction is the character and industrial patina that reconverted warehouses and factories offer; but a larger reason is the flexibility engendered by such open loft spaces.

Proof of the wide appeal of the loft is its popularity as a marketing tool for residential developments that are anything but reconverted industrial spaces. So many newly built condominiums in Miami, for instance, tout loft-style interiors as one of the biggest reasons to buy. Why? Because the open, minimally programmed interiors that are the lasting legacy of loft living accommodate a variety of functions, family arrangements, and lifestyles. The flexibility that comes with such open, airy interiors is the key to accommodating the specific requests and unforeseen needs of the modern-day family.

Today's architects are liberating the loft from the confines of the city, pushing freedom and flexibility to new levels in stand-alone houses. These homes are as much an evolution of the modernist free plan as an evolution of an urban typology developed only relatively recently. Whether you trace its pedigree to Mies or Manhattan, contemporary permutations of free-plan living run a wide gamut, from tough urban bunkers to Shigeru Ban's provocatively titled Naked House in Kawagoe, Japan, a pristine light-filled structure. This simple box wrapped in translucent plastic is the ultimate blank slate. Not content to simply create an open-plan interior for flexibility's sake, Ban designed four moveable rooms—actually boxes on large casters—that can be rolled around the lofty house as needed, or even outdoors. The rolling rooms, outfitted with tatami mats and sliding screens, are used primarily as bedrooms, but the tops of the boxes are suitable as play or study areas for children. It's an experiment in flexible living, to be sure, but a successful one.

So many of the projects featured in this book incorporate their own take on the loft typology, each to particular effect. The Fletcher Page House by Australian architect Glenn Murcutt (page 16) is nothing so much as a minimalist shed in the country. The goal behind open-plan living in this house is the desire to create a permeable structure to bring light, view, and air into a quiet retreat. A family vacation compound on the Gulf Coast of Florida designed by Toshiko Mori (page 142) looked to unstructured interiors as a reflection of the unstructured, relaxed lifestyle its occupants wanted to lead there. German architect Werner Sobek's home in Stuttgart (page 186) is an absolutely minimalist glass box. Sobek elected not to divide the floor plates into distinct rooms so as not to impede the flow of space and light throughout.

Accessible retreats and second homes

One carryover of the new widespread interest in domesticity—not to mention the financial appeal of real estate investment—is that second homes are no longer seen as trophy items for the wealthy. As people lead busier workweeks in the city, weekend houses and vacation homes are seen as necessary escapes from the pressures of daily life. With the loosening of attitudes toward second homes have come innovative alternatives to the traditional beach or mountain getaway. Take, for example, Australian architect Drew Heath's compact cabin in the rural brush outside Sydney (page 88). Built for a busy urban couple, the house boils down "weekend" to its barest essentials: The house is little more than a well-designed architectonic tent, with outdoor plumbing and little indoor space. But for the clients, it's exactly what they need to escape their city lives.

Above: Shigeru Ban's Naked House in Kawagoe, Japan, creates the ultimate in flexibility with rolling rooms on casters.

High-end vacation homes have hardly gone out of fashion. On the contrary: As homeowners become increasingly savvy about design, modern houses by well-known architects are themselves becoming collectible pedigreed objects. Perhaps one of the more slickly publicized examples is the project in New York's famed Hamptons called The Houses at Sagaponac. The brainchild of developer Coco Brown and architect Richard Meier, the project is a speculative development of thirty-four houses, each designed by a well-known architect picked by Meier. Among those selected were old-guard architects such as Zaha Hadid, Philip Johnson, Michael Graves, and Richard Rogers, as well as a younger generation, including Steven Holl, Richard Gluckman, and Shigeru Ban. Their houses sit on roughly one- to two-acre plots and cost several million dollars each. The development puts a premium on individual design over community. When they are all eventually built, the houses will have little relationship among themselves or with the site, a flat stretch of land surrounded by unappealing scrub oak; they will look more like pavilions at a world's fair. But the appeal of the famous architects behind them will make the houses highly desirable commodities.

The Sagaponac project is not the only one to market high-profile modern architecture as a means of selling real estate. Meier's controversial condominiums in Manhattan and Philippe Starck's worldwide Yoo! franchise with UK developer John Hitchcox are just two examples. These developments underscore a potentially hazardous trend in residential real estate: homes that put a greater value on the fame of the architect who designed them than on the design itself, and how that may or may not be appropriate for its owners. It's difficult to imagine architects of this caliber creating spec houses, but that's exactly what most of these projects are: off-the-shelf homes conceived for an unknown client. Hiring an architect to create a one-off home has its price, but the resulting home meets very specific needs and desires. It's the equivalent of a couture gown versus a ready-to-wear frock, though in the case of some of these developments, the off-the-rack design may not cost that much less than a custom creation.

China's newfound wealth and its recent interest in architecture by architects from abroad spawned its own version of the Houses at Sagaponac. Commune by the Great Wall is not dissimilar from the Hamptons project, although its name puts a more egalitarian spin on the idea of collectible high-end houses. (Another difference is that the units built as part of the first phase of the Commune project are operated as a high-end boutique hotel.) Developer Zhang Xin, of SOHO China, invited twelve architects from Asia to design a series of hillside villas near the famous Great Wall, about an hour outside of Beijing. Architects such as Kengo Kuma and Shigeru Ban created a disparate group of houses, each of which addresses its own functional and conceptual issues. For instance, the Split House designed by Chinese architect Yung Ho Chang of Atelier Feichang Jianzhu reinterprets the traditional Beijing courtyard house made of environmentally friendly rammed earth and laminated wood. Chang adapted the traditionally urban typology to the rural setting of the Commune, adjusting the two wings of the V-shaped floor plan specifically to the position of existing trees in the space between them. He sees the house as a prototypical model: The exact position of the two legs of the house, which separate public and private functions within each wing, can be changed according to its site and its occupants' needs. Thus, the V shape can be turned into two parallel structures separated by an outdoor space, two conjoined wings, an L-shaped house, a T-shaped plan, or any other combination. The ecological benefit of the rammed earth construction is that the house could be easily and cleanly demolished—if one would actually want to destroy such a house.

Tangible innovation

Perhaps the most readily apparent advancements in modern houses are the physical ones: materials, building systems, and construction techniques. This is the focus of the houses featured in section 03. Like Yung Ho Chang's Split House at the Great Wall commune, architects are showing increased concern with how their houses can be recycled at the end of their life spans, even though it seems unlikely that clients would

Top: A house by Zaha Hadid is one of the speculative homes designed by famous architects for the Houses at Sagaponac development on Long Island, New York.

Above: The Split House, part of the Commune by the Great Wall development in China, features a flexible floor plan designed by Yung Ho Chang.

make the ease and environmental benefits of a home's demolition a top priority. Architect Werner Sobek touts how easily the modular steel frame of his house in Stuttgart can be taken apart as much as how quickly it was built.

Sobek's house is one of the most technologically adventurous projects in this book. The architect treated it as a live-in experiment on just about every aspect of its construction: its thermally efficient glass skin, its snap-in-place steel frame, its hands-free control of everything from the heating and cooling systems to cabinets and doors. Such a complete and orchestrated combination of sophisticated systems and materials makes a compelling case for homes that carefully analyze overall performance, not just a few high-tech bells and whistles. However, the element that may offer the most relevance to the current crush of high energy prices is the way the house absorbs, stores, and rereleases solar energy as radiant heat in winter.

Indeed, houses that conserve and even generate at least some of their own heat and power seem the most genuinely innovative—more commonsensical, really—given the geopolitical tensions that have caused the price of oil and power to spike dramatically in the last several years. The last major global oil crisis in the 1970s prompted a short-lived attempt at what we would now call sustainable architecture: so-called solar homes that used passive techniques for heating and cooling. The movement was ultimately unsuccessful, and "solar homes" went the way of disco and polyester pantsuits. One of the many reasons that what sounded like a promising change in home design never quite took off is that the architects behind them never mastered the integration of technology and esthetics.

Home technology has evolved significantly since the energy crises of the 1970s. Advanced building products have become affordable and available: More efficient heating and cooling systems, for example, and windows and glazing systems that reduce heat gain are all taken for granted. But one major advancement is that architects have learned how to better turn state-of-the-art technology into appealing architecture. They have borrowed a page from the sophisticated industrial, commercial, and even institutional buildings of high-tech architects like Norman Foster, Renzo Piano, and Richard Rogers. Technology aside, the sleek glass skin and meticulous detailing of Sobek's home make for an esthetically appealing house, a crystalline box of which Mies van der Rohe would surely approve.

Another compelling project that elevates energy-saving and energy-generating technology to new levels of design sophistication is the Colorado Court housing project in Santa Monica, California, designed by Pugh + Scarpa Architecture. The architects report that this urban complex of forty-four single-room-occupancy apartments is one of the first residential projects of its kind in the United States to be 100 percent energy independent—that is, the building generates more power than it consumes. Its energy-conscious elements are integral to the design: Power-generating photovoltaic panels are part of the exterior, not add-ons. In fact, the south facades are dominated by arrangements of photovoltaic panels. Pugh + Scarpa used technology to create strong architecture. A similar strategy is unfolding on partner Lawrence Scarpa's own home, the Solar Umbrella. Scarpa wrapped photovoltaic panels that will generate all of the home's electrical needs from the south facade onto a canopy-like roof inspired by the streamlined modern style of Paul Rudolph. Again, form and technology merge to create elegant, functional, and energy-efficient architecture.

It could be debated whether the Straw Bale House designed by London architects Sara Wigglesworth and Jeremy Till (page 192) for themselves is as efficient—or as elegant—as Pugh + Scarpa's experiment in solar-powered housing in Los Angeles. But it is certainly innovative—perhaps the most original and inventive of all the houses featured in this book, with walls made of bundled straw and concrete-filled sandbags and gabion pillars of recycled concrete chunks bound by wire cages. Each choice of material and technique responds to a specific need: extra insulation, soundproofing, and an absorptive structure to soften the constant rumble of passing trains. The sum total of these disparate elements may not be a seamlessly coherent design, but they give the house an active, lively aura of experimentation.

Top: Colorado Court, a housing project in Santa Monica, California, by Pugh + Scarpa, generates its own power with photovoltaic panels that are integrated into the design of the facades.

Above: Architect Samuel Mockbee's Rural Studio designed Lucy's House in Mason's Bend, Alabama, with stacked walls of donated carpets.

The late architect, educator, and humanitarian Samuel Mockbee was no stranger to using unorthodox materials to make dignified, well-designed buildings for some of the poorest residents of the American Deep South. In the hands of Mockbee and his students and followers at the much admired Rural Studio at Auburn University, car windshields, salvaged road signs, and old tires became viable materials for building astonishingly inexpensive—and surprisingly handsome—houses, schools, and churches. One of Mockbee's last built projects, Lucy's House in rural Mason's Bend, Alabama, is a colorful home with walls of stacked recycled carpet tiles—72,000 of them—which were donated by a carpet manufacturer. To give the layered carpet tiles some structural integrity, Mockbee concealed steel rods within the striated walls to support the pitched roof above. Like all Rural Studio projects, the cost was astonishingly low: in this case, about $30,000. If necessity is the mother of invention, Mockbee's experiments in frugality are some of the most inventive buildings anywhere. They have humor, wit, and strong design ideas, but no pretension or high cost.

Material innovation is not always undertaken in the name of sustainability or philanthropy; sometimes it is pure poetry of form that drives an architect's experiments, as houses throughout this book demonstrate. Kengo Kuma's Bamboo Wall House (page 166) is an essay in using slender woody reeds to create quiet, contemplative spaces. MADA s.p.a.m.'s Father's House on Jade Mountain (page 178) explores the strong texture of polished pebbles set into walls of concrete. Other houses create strong personalities with a single material: Rick Joy's Tubac House in the Arizona desert (page 50) and Shim-Sutcliffe's Weathering Steel House in Toronto (page 42) explore the sculptural qualities of rusty steel in radically different climates and contexts. In a private home he designed in Chicago (page 220), Tadao Ando polishes his already pristine signature material: poured-in-place concrete.

The titles of the book's sections acknowledge just a few of the issues of importance to contemporary architects and their clients, but they are by no means the only issues at play in modern houses. The groupings are by necessity constricting, as some houses would make an equally strong contribution to multiple categories. For instance, Richard Meier's Neugebauer House was placed in section 03 (page 204) because of its attention to environmental controls. Meier's sleek waterfront house seamlessly integrates elegant built-in sunscreens that minimize heat gain on the south- and west-facing glass facades. But the house is also worth noting for its skillful separation of public living spaces, bedrooms, and services. Meier layered the house into three distinct zones: a service corridor at the back, living areas and bedrooms along the waterfront side (the two wings are separated by an interior foyer and exterior patio), and bathrooms and service spaces in between. One can completely isolate the bedroom wing from guests without them feeling that the house has been partitioned. The circulation along the service corridor lets the occupants move freely from, say, the bedrooms to the kitchen without traversing the living/dining room. The occupants also have direct access to their bedrooms from the pool, again allowing them to get to their private quarters without dripping water on the floor in the home's more formal public spaces.

Rediscovering Prefab

It would be impossible to survey contemporary modern houses without delving into one of the most talked about trends in residential architecture: prefabrication. Pre-built homes are hardly a new idea. Numerous architects in the first half of the twentieth century tried their hand at changing the domestic landscape with prefabricated homes. Jean Prouvé, Buckminster Fuller, Walter Gropius, Albert Frey, and other pioneering modernists designed streamlined prefabricated houses that furthered the Modern Movement's initial mandate of building architecture with a sense of social revolution. Some were more unconventional than others: Frey's Aluminaire House of 1930 looked like an International Style house that just happened to be prefabricated, but Fuller's famous Dymaxion dome was more extreme, perhaps a turnoff to prospective buyers. The mass-produced housing movement soon lost momentum, and by the 1950s the notion of

Top: Buckminster Fuller's Dymaxion dome, first developed in the late 1920s, was an early experiment in prefabricated home design.

Above: IKEA's popular BoKlok homes are cozier, more traditional versions of the prefab house.

building communities of prefab homes had completely fizzled out. Factory-made housing became the province of mobile homes and recreational vehicles, not serious modern architecture.

Things have changed in recent years. Consumers have come to expect affordable well-designed modern style in everything from teapots and toasters to computers and cars. The logical extension of this democratization of design is affordable, accessible architecture for buyers who want an architect-designed modern home but can't or don't want to pay the cost of a one-off creation. There is a growing market to fill the significant gap between developer housing and specially commissioned homes, and architects around the world are rushing to fill the need with houses that incorporate factory-made or preassembled parts, which offer lower costs and higher construction precision than site-built homes.

European architects are leading the prefab movement, perhaps spurred on by Europe's higher population densities and housing costs. Sweden's mass-market modern retailer IKEA has been building pre-assembled BoKlok (or "Live Smart") houses for several years. In Finland, more than 90 percent of single-family homes are prefabricated. Some projects have a decidedly prefab appearance—metal boxes that look like they just came off the delivery truck—while others, including the Swedish-country BoKlok houses and Finnish architects Heikkinen Komonen's prefab Touch House look deceivingly custom-built.

The prefab trend is catching on in the United States, although there are few designs on the market and no real efficient production and distribution system yet in place to make it a widespread phenomenon. (Architect Rocio Romero chose to base her prefab-housing operation in Missouri in large part because it is equidistant from both the East and West coasts of the United States, where presumably most of her clients are located.) Negative connotations with mobile homes and generally unappealing housing are also likely holding back consumers. But as more attractive and feasible designs come on line, the situation is changing. Romero's LV Home Kit, Brooklyn architect Craig Konyk's up!house, and the weeHouse by Alchemy Architects in St. Paul, Minnesota, are all striking modern prefab homes already on the market.

Perhaps the most radical proposition in the world of prefab housing is for developing compact living units from used shipping containers. As extreme as the idea sounds, a number of architects are exploring the possibility of turning empty containers into dwellings. Proponents of the trend point out that redundant industrial trailers are readily accessible (after the goods they contain are unloaded, most containers sit idle in the world's ports), inexpensive, and completely portable. In theory, one could ship one's self and one's home from one location to another. Even though trailers are not recyclable commodities, turning them into housing is a good way to put a redundant material to good use.

One of the first architects to champion shipping containers was the New York firm LOT/EK, who have turned other industrial detritus such as fuel tanks into funky, hard-edged living spaces. LOT/EK's most comprehensive proposal for recycled container living is their Mobile Dwelling Unit. LOT/EK cut up a single container and extruded sections of its corrugated skin to create a small kitchen, sleeping area, and dining space projecting from the fiberglass-finished interior.

Though they helped pioneer the medium, LOT/EK are not the only architects exploring the potential of cargo containers as spaces for living. Australian architect Sean Godsell proposed emergency relief structures made of a single container shaded by a sturdy pitched roof. Jennifer Siegal's Venice, California, practice, appropriately called the Office of Mobile Design, also designs affordable and moveable constructions from truck trailers and shipping containers.

These adventurous homes built with unorthodox and overlooked materials are at the exploratory edge of the new modern house. Insight and innovation is alive and well in many forms, some subtle, others extreme. The houses in this volume chart that ongoing exploration. They represent just a tiny cross-section through the immense landscape of contemporary homes, but capture the most significant new trends taking shape. It's an important moment for the way we live now, and for the modern house of the future.

Top: A computer rendering of the all-steel up!house, a prefabricated, 100 percent recyclable house designed by Craig Konyk.

Above: LOT/EK's Mobile Dwelling Unit prototype offers flexible, portable accommodation in a recycled shipping container.

01 merging inside and out

One of the Modern Movement's most enduring legacies is its dissolution of the traditional boundaries between interior and exterior space. The pioneers of Modernism radically reconceived the very notion of space, from a subtractive process of carving voids from solid walls of poché to the containment of an endless flow of space by the planes of floors, walls, and ceilings. As architects such as Le Corbusier and Mies van der Rohe liberated a building's structure from its skin, the walls that once divided inside from outside, now structurally unnecessary, vanished, replaced by diaphanous skins of glass. The outdoors became part of the interior, and interior space was allowed to expand beyond a building's boundaries.

Nowhere was the disappearance of exterior walls more revolutionary than in the realm of the private house. For centuries, the home was cherished as the ultimate personal refuge, primarily designed for psychological and physical shelter from the world outside. Imagine the shock in 1915, when Le Corbusier proposed his Maison Dom-ino, a structurally simple house created with two thin slabs of concrete supported on a grid of concrete columns. Since the columns would be providing the necessary structural support for the house, the exterior walls could all but disappear. Were he not practicing and theorizing architecture in cold, damp Paris, he might have suggested wrapping the house in a lightweight fabric curtain instead of a thin curtain wall. Still, the architect broke important new ground with the notion that the interiors of a house could extend far beyond its walls, with glass or with nothing at all.

Mies van der Rohe gave elegant form to Le Corbusier's ideas when he designed the Farnsworth House in Plano, Illinois, which was completed in 1951. The home's interior bleeds out through huge panes of glass, the only barrier to the outdoors. Low partitions extending to the ceiling keep views of the prairie uninterrupted from every space in the house. Decades before the urban loft became the ultimate embodiment of free-plan living, Mies created an urbane "loft" in the country with an open floor plan and transparent walls.

Contemporary architects continue to explore the possibilities of merging inside and outside space first contemplated by these twentieth-century pioneers. Technology has advanced far beyond the structural innovations that first made it possible to throw open the walls, so to speak, but the groundbreaking open-plan houses of Mies, Le Corbusier, and other early modernists remain important sources of inspiration. The Spanish architect Alberto Campo Baeza took inspiration specifically from the Farnsworth House in his design for the De Blas House outside Madrid (page 36). Campo Baeza perched a minimalist enclosure—slender steel columns and a thin roof, painted white like Mies's iconic Illinois house—atop a concrete plinth containing the main living spaces. Beneath the steel pavilion is a transparent box of floor-to-ceiling glass where the only function is quiet contemplation. The space within the glass box draws in views of the surrounding hillsides, the viewer's eye drawn out by the long horizontal planes of the roof.

Architects working in warm, dry locations have a distinct advantage over those designing houses for cold, rainy climates. Shelter from the occasional storm may be necessary, but shutters and doors don't have to be drawn all the time. In the Weiss House in the tropical desert of Cabo San Lucas, Mexico (page 22), New York architect Steven Harris took full advantage of the possibility of making truly outdoor rooms. Some spaces in the house, which is perched high above the Pacific Ocean, are elegant, well-appointed interiors with large sliding glass doors that create rooms without walls. Others are literally conceived as outdoor rooms: spaces shaded by nothing more than a thin concrete roof. Parisian architects Sandra Barclay and Jean-Pierre Crousse took a similar approach in their Casa Equis in coastal Cañete, Peru (page 68), a place where rainfall is virtually unknown. They kept the circulation completely open to the elements and made a living and dining room that seamlessly extends onto a large oceanfront terrace and pool, thanks to retractable glass walls. In rural Tubac, Arizona, architect Rick Joy designed a house with large window walls that open every room to the dramatic desert landscape (page 50). A large opening cut into the rusty steel wall frames a slice of the landscape like a painting mounted on the wall.

Even in cold climates, integrating indoor and outdoor space can be a desirable proposition. The seaside Koehler House in New Brunswick, Canada, by Julie Snow (page 60) and Shim-Sutcliffe's Weathering Steel House in suburban Toronto (page 42) demonstrate that changing weather throughout the year animates the home when the architecture embraces the outdoors. For its part, Shim-Sutcliffe made sure that ponds and reflecting pools abutting the home's large glass doors don't need unattractive plastic covers in winter; steam billowing off the water in winter creates a beautiful view from indoors, especially with snow on the ground. At the Koehler House, high above the harsh but spectacular New Brunswick coast, Julie Snow designed sliding wood panels that the owners can draw closed in front of large glass walls to create an added sense of enclosure.

Design elements that adapt to changes in the weather or the owner's desire for privacy are the most innovative responses to integrating interiors with the exterior. Architect Sean Godsell designed a simple wooden beach house (page 30) that changes, chameleon-like, when it occupants prop open the panels of thin cedar slats of the exterior skin.

Clearly, architects are still fascinated with the possibility of confounding interior and exterior space to make richer experiences in the private home. They continue the Modern tradition of non-tradition, of breaking down old-fashioned barriers between inside and out.

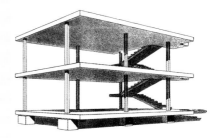

Opposite: Julie Snow's Koehler House on the Atlantic Coast of Canada interprets early modernist ideas of opening homes to the landscape.

Top: Mies van der Rohe's Farnsworth House (1951) remains an icon of visual continuity between indoors and outdoors.

Above: Le Corbusier's Maison Dom-Ino of 1915 offered a similar strategy decades earlier.

The Pritzker Prize–winning Australian architect Glenn Murcutt is known for sleek, gossamer structures that temper the structural clarity and simplicity of Mies van der Rohe with an appreciation of native Aboriginal structures. Far from a regional modernist, Murcutt's primary goal is to draw from the lessons of Australia's Aboriginal and early European structures to make modern buildings that respond to their surroundings. As the architect has said, "I'm interested in an architecture that continually acknowledges the physical and climatic character of its site; that recognizes the sorts of changes in scale we experience when we move from the inside to the outside." The Fletcher Page House in Australia's pastoral Kangaroo Valley, 170 kilometers (105 miles) south of Sydney, continues Murcutt's exploration into houses that integrate indoors and out.

The home's simple, straightforward form—a low-slung bar crowned by a thin, angled metal roof with deep overhangs—recalls many of Murcutt's earlier houses, including the Meager House in Bowral, New South Wales (1992), and his sublime Simpson Lee House in Mount Wilson, New South Wales (1994). Murcutt prefers this long, narrow form because he finds it relates well to the horizontal vistas and landscapes of Australia's open spaces. The Fletcher Page House sits squarely on a concrete slab on grade, in a clearing in a wooded site. The 33.25-meter-long (109-feet-long) house is a continuous volume with separate functions demarcated by partitions that stop short of the inclined metal roof. (Angled glass clerestories provide some acoustic privacy between spaces while letting light flow through uninterrupted.) The entry is located at the center of the 4.31-meter-wide (14-feet-wide) bar. To one side of the small entry vestibule is a bedroom, bathroom, studio, and garage; to the other is the open kitchen, living, and dining space, the master bedroom, and a veranda (a typical Australian covered porch).

Murcutt designed the bar as a visually and environmentally permeable structure with openings tailored to the sunlight, air, and views. In the southern hemisphere, northern exposures are the sunny ones, so the architect provided deep roof overhangs to shade a continuous ribbon of clerestory windows extending the full length of the north elevation. He fitted north-facing windows with louvers and added retractable wood shutters over small windows that help cross-ventilate the space. On the shadier south facade, Murcutt opened up the house as much as possible. This orientation also has the best views of the surrounding valley landscape. Large glass doors along the loft-like living/dining area slide open to make the space feel like part of the outdoors—as if an entire wall of the house had been removed. Murcutt added insect screens to make "outdoor living" more comfortable inside and sliding wood shutters for added privacy.

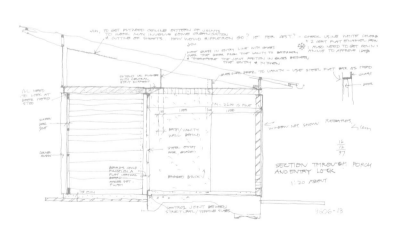

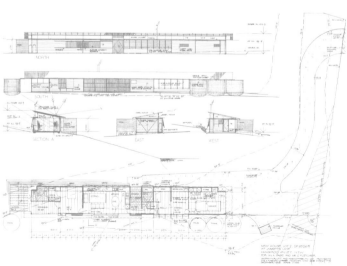

The architect kept the south-facing walls thin so as to make the entire elevation feel almost immaterial, so he relegated fixed functions to the north facade, where he wanted fewer openings to keep out direct sunlight. Murcutt placed plumbing and other infrastructure along the northern edge of each room. The bathrooms, laundry facilities in the garage, a built-in desk in the guest room, a bench sink in the studio, the kitchen sink and storage cabinets, and the wood-burning fireplace in the living area all occupy the northern flank of the house.

The Fletcher Page House is remarkably simple but well thought-out, providing maximum flexibility but keeping in mind considerations of climate and view. The house reinterprets the traditional Australian veranda in a thoroughly modern way, as Murcutt does in many of his houses. In this case, the veranda is not an appendage to the house, but the house itself. It's the perfect space from which to regard the outdoors while being part of nature.

Previous spread: The shadier, south facade is open to the outdoors as much as possible.

Opposite, top: The low-slung, single-story house opens up to the sun with a continuous band of clerestory windows beneath the angled roof. Louvers and retractable shutters provide shade.

Opposite, bottom: cross-section (left); elevations, sections, and floor plan (right).

Above: The interior is an open loft-like space divided by partitions that stop short of the inclined ceiling. The main living space at the center of the house contains a kitchen, dining area, and living room that opens to the outdoors with large sliding glass doors.

Opposite, top left: The roof
above the open living-dining
area and kitchen slopes
up to create a clerestory that
extends the length of the house.

Opposite, top right: The roof
overhang reveals Murcutt's
attention to detailing.

Opposite, bottom: The west
elevation reveals how compact
the house is.

Above: Glass doors between
the bedroom and the rest of the
house ensure light can flow
freely throughout the interior.

weiss house

Steven Harris Architects
Cabo San Lucas, Mexico 2002

Cabo San Lucas, at the tip of Mexico's Baja California peninsula, is a tropical desert, one of the few places in the world where a true desert meets the ocean. Aside from the dramatic landscapes—rocky cliffs with cactus and desert blooms overlooking the Pacific—the lack of humidity and much rainfall makes it an attractive place to build. One can spend much of the time outdoors, and in fact live in truly outdoor rooms open to the elements.

New York architect Steven Harris created a retreat on the southern end of the peninsula that takes full advantage of the delightfully arid climate. Working with noted landscape designer Margie Ruddick, Harris designed a 9,000-square-foot ensemble of indoor and outdoor spaces woven into desert gardens and boulders on a rocky cliff that plunges 250 feet to the deep blue Pacific Ocean. The house has stylishly furnished rooms that open to the ocean view with floor-to-ceiling glass walls, others that open completely to the outdoors with retractable glass doors—and some with no walls at all. Harris's design is one of those rare houses where the architecture is strong enough to create its own identity and personality, but respectful enough of its precarious site that the architecture feels deferential to it. Architecture, landscape, and views feed on and enhance each other.

Entering the house from the top of the cliff, above the flat rooftops of the house, one descends along a rough stone staircase and arrives at a small foyer. The foyer opens onto an arid courtyard landscaped with desert blooms and chunky boulders. Harris divided the home's ample square footage among three separate volumes arranged around the courtyard to maximize privacy and views. An L-shaped wing at the southern edge of the site contains a master suite, gym, and media room. Facing the master suite across the courtyard are the main living spaces: an open-air dining room, kitchen, and an oceanfront living room enclosed in large panes of hurricane-resistant glass. The third volume is an outdoor living area—a truly outdoor room without walls or windows. The living room, a simple open pavilion with a flat concrete roof

Previous spread: A lap pool extends from the study and outdoor living room above to the Pacific Ocean.

Opposite: Buried into a rocky cliff, the living pavilion features large panes of hurricane-resistant glass shaded by a deep roof overhang. Below the living room is one of three guest rooms.

Above: The pavilion containing the living and dining rooms is one of three structures surrounding a desert courtyard.

Left: Site plan.

atop slender steel columns, floats above a partially bermed study defined by a thick wall of native Mexican stone. Large sliding glass doors in the study open onto a lap pool that points toward the blue horizon of the Pacific. The three guest rooms are extremely private, buried into the rocky hillside and reached by stone steps leading down from the courtyard. One is located beneath the living/dining room, the others are beneath the master suite.

Harris kept the materials basic: reinforced concrete, a specialty of the local construction industry; native Mexican stone; and glass. But the play of light and water throughout the house is anything but simple. Strip skylights wash the walls of exposed stone with tropical sunlight. Harris embedded glass rods into the east-facing concrete wall to create patterned rings of light when the early morning sun hits that particular exposure. A water runnel above a skylit shower creates a shimmery pattern of light on the floor of the shower. All of these details make an intimate connection between the architecture and the site, between the earth and the sky. In these tropical latitudes, however, controlling excess sun is more important than creating poetic plays of light. Harris made sure to shade indoor and outdoor rooms with deep roof overhangs. The projecting concrete roof

planes let him open up as much of the exterior surface as possible, to bring the views inside.

The home's sophisticated interiors belie the simplicity of the construction methods. The clients told Harris they wanted "martini modern" style, which is to say from the mid-century modern heyday of Palm Springs, California. The architect and interior designer Lucien Rees-Roberts complied, with elegantly furnished rooms that strike a provocative counterpoint to tough rocky cliff into which the house is built. The effect is most striking in the dining room, where a grand piano and an elegant chandelier above the dining table seem dangerously exposed to the elements when the wall of glass doors slides open.

Above: The floor-to-ceiling glass enclosing the formal living room blends indoor and outdoor space.

Opposite, top: At night, the compound appears as a series of brightly lit lanterns crowning a rocky hillside above the Pacific.

Opposite, bottom: A path between the outdoor living room, at left, and the master suite, at right, acts as an open-air corridor.

Opposite, top left: Full-height
glass opens the living room to a
view of the Pacific Ocean.

Opposite, top right: The
house includes an open-air
shower framed in a rough
wall of local stone.

Opposite, bottom: Retractable
glass walls completely open
the formal dining room to the
central courtyard.

Above: The lap pool is framed
by walls of stone and concrete
that screen out other parts of
the house.

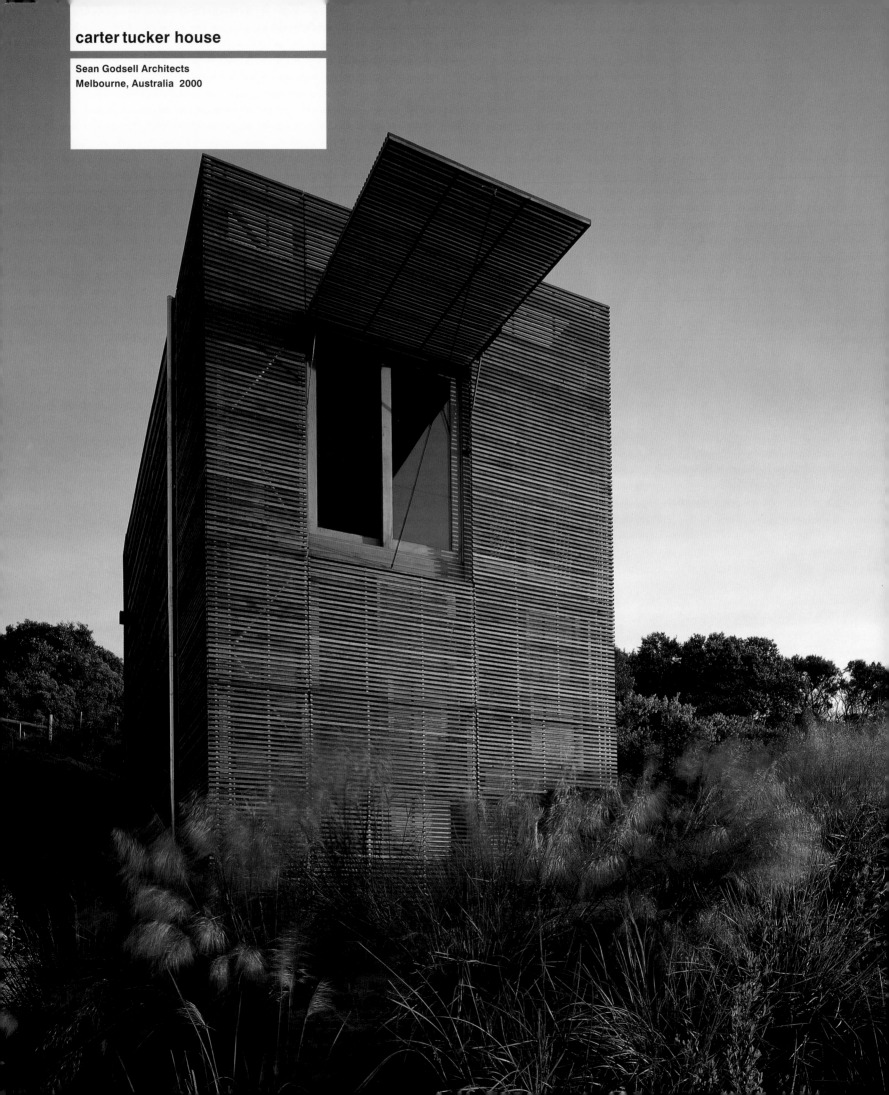

carter tucker house

Sean Godsell Architects
Melbourne, Australia 2000

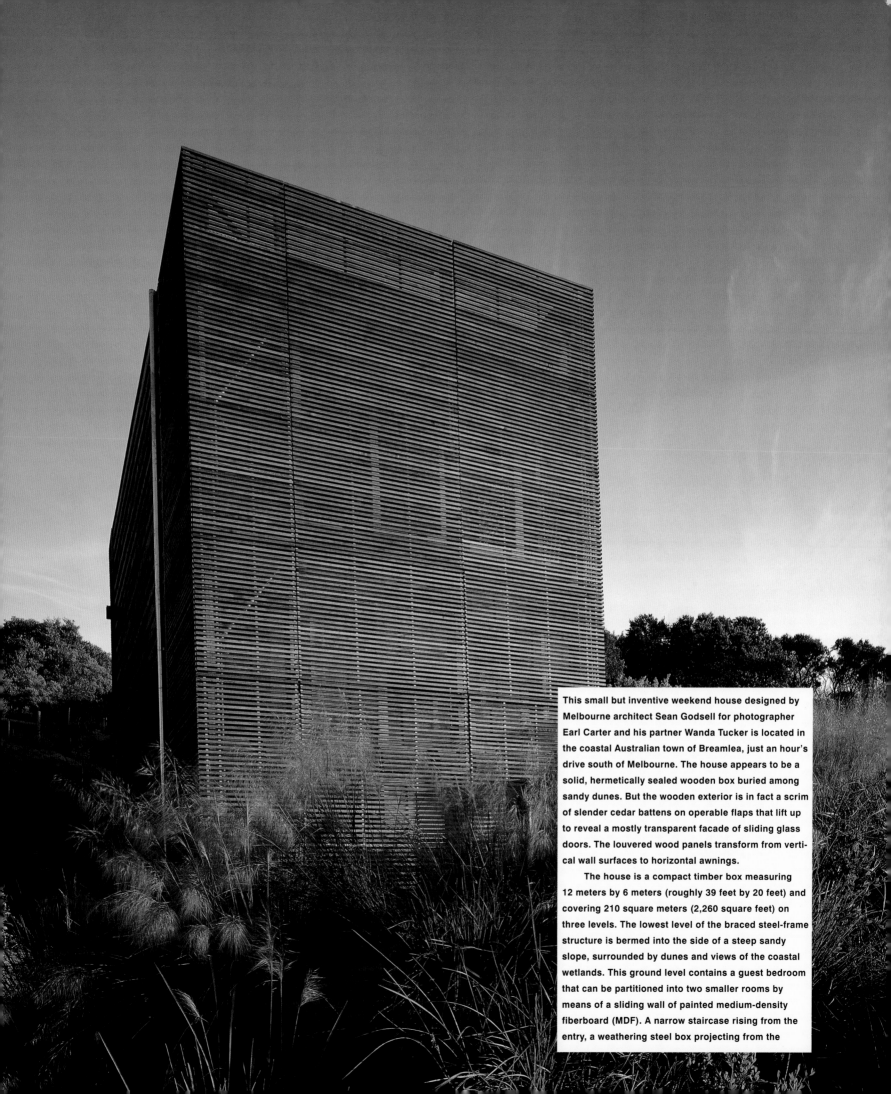

This small but inventive weekend house designed by Melbourne architect Sean Godsell for photographer Earl Carter and his partner Wanda Tucker is located in the coastal Australian town of Breamlea, just an hour's drive south of Melbourne. The house appears to be a solid, hermetically sealed wooden box buried among sandy dunes. But the wooden exterior is in fact a scrim of slender cedar battens on operable flaps that lift up to reveal a mostly transparent facade of sliding glass doors. The louvered wood panels transform from vertical wall surfaces to horizontal awnings.

The house is a compact timber box measuring 12 meters by 6 meters (roughly 39 feet by 20 feet) and covering 210 square meters (2,260 square feet) on three levels. The lowest level of the braced steel-frame structure is bermed into the side of a steep sandy slope, surrounded by dunes and views of the coastal wetlands. This ground level contains a guest bedroom that can be partitioned into two smaller rooms by means of a sliding wall of painted medium-density fiberboard (MDF). A narrow staircase rising from the entry, a weathering steel box projecting from the

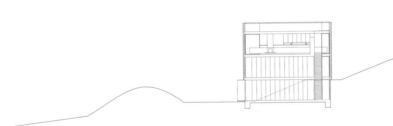

Previous spread: When shutters are popped open (left), the simple wooden box takes on a whole new character.

Opposite: A wall of storage cabinets behind the dining area floats in front of the louvered exterior.

Top left: A narrow staircase connects the home's three levels.

Top right: On the top floor, glass doors behind the facade of wood louvers slide open

to create a permeable skin. A fold-down staircase leads to a roof deck.

Above: A section shows how the house is bermed into a sandy hillside.

otherwise all-wood exterior, leads up to the owners' bedroom on the second floor and the main living spaces on the top level. Like the guest room below, the master bedroom can be partitioned with a sliding MDF wall to create a separate private sitting area. On the top floor, where the owners also keep a daylight photography studio, a staircase between the living and dining areas folds down for access to a roof deck.

The interiors are minimalist and loft-like, with hardwood floors, walls paneled in horizontal cedar boards, and little else. The primary element of the house is light: The intensity, brightness, and patterns of sunlight through the louvers change constantly as the natural light outside changes. There is a strong Asian quality to the house, especially in its simple wooden surfaces and mutable spaces with sliding walls. The permeable louvered enclosure also reveals a variation on the traditional Australian veranda, typically a long outdoor porch attached to the house that functions as an open-air anteroom and an outdoor living room in warm weather. In this project, the entire house is a giant veranda created by doors and screens that completely open the indoors to the outside world.

The house has an interesting "both/and" personality: It is both shut out and removed from its surroundings and it is also extremely open to the outdoors. In a

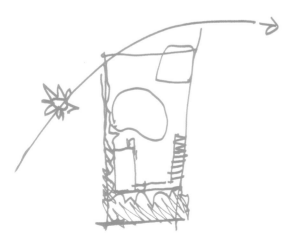

Above: A fold-down staircase between the living and dining areas leads to a roof deck with views of the coast. Furnishings are kept away from the exterior walls to keep the perimeter as open as possible.

Left: Sketch of the sun's trajectory around the house.

Opposite: Operable flaps of varying dimensions pop open to reveal sliding glass doors. When fixed, the flaps double as sunscreens or awnings.

sense, the exterior skin is hardly a skin at all. When the flaps are lifted and the glass doors opened, the house becomes completely permeable. It also changes character dramatically, from introverted bunker to lighthearted playhouse in the dunes.

Godsell has received accolades for his design for FutureShack, an environmentally conscientious shelter for emergency and relief housing constructed from a recycled shipping container. The Carter Tucker house is not prefabricated or made of preassembled parts, but it shares a similar attitude about material efficiency, flexibility, and simple economy of means.

de blas house

Alberto Campo Baeza
Sevilla la Nueva, Spain 2000

The Madrid-based architect Alberto Campo Baeza is known for elegantly restrained buildings that create powerful architecture from simple, often whitewashed volumes and light. His muscular minimalism, all in Spain, has received notice from the likes of former Gucci design director Tom Ford. In the rural outskirts of Madrid, Campo Baeza designed a strikingly minimalist house that makes a strong visual impression despite the fact that it seems to have barely intruded on the landscape.

The 370-square-meter (3,976-square-foot) house is really two separate structures. All of the living spaces are contained within a 9-meter-by-27-meter (30-foot-by-89-foot) concrete box bermed into the slope so that on one side only small square windows punched into the upper reaches of the concrete enclosure are visible above the ground. (On the opposite side, the full height of the structure is exposed, allowing larger windows, as well as the front door, to overlook the surrounding valley.) The rough concrete box becomes a solid plinth atop which Campo Baeza placed a delicate steel structure with frameless glass walls, next to a swimming pool that is as much a reflective water feature as it is a functional recreational element. The structure seems to float like an abstract box above the brusque hillside.

The lower level contains all of the home's required functions in a rigidly orthogonal, symmetrical arrangement. Without much fanfare, the discrete entry door near the center of the concrete base opens directly into the living room. The rear wall of the living space conceals a narrow staircase that leads to the glass pavilion above—a poetic metaphor of moving up from darkness to light, from shelter and functionalism to contemplation and enlightenment—behind which is the kitchen. To the right of the living room is a study and a bedroom and bath; to the left is the dining room and another bedroom and bath. The architect reserved the best light and view for the living and sleeping spaces, and put the kitchen and bathroom along the darker, partially buried north wall. A single south-facing window in each of the living and bedroom spaces makes them feel brighter than one would expect in what is essentially a concrete box buried into the hill. An extra-large window makes the living room the brightest space of all.

Upstairs, the glass pavilion is a stark contrast to the enclosed sheltered living quarters. Campo Baeza did not assign a specific function to the lightweight structure other than silent contemplation of the surrounding landscape through large panes of frameless glass beneath a white steel canopy. There are really two rooms: the space defined by the glass walls and the larger area demarcated by the deep overhanging roof atop slender steel columns. Standing on the concrete surface, one feels as if at ground level, not on the rooftop of an underground home.

1
mountain + tree

2
to stablish a
          platform

3
to carve   to house.   hot
                          cold

← STEREOTOMIC

4
to cover   ... it is raining

to plan   ... it is windy
              ←TECTONIC.

stereotomic + tectonic =
= ARCHITECTURE.

Previous spread: The textured concrete walls enclosing the lower-level living spaces blend with the arid hillside.

Opposite, far left: Conceptual studies of the home's position in the landscape.

Opposite, top: With its neutral palette and minimal materials, the house and rooftop structure recede into the landscape.

Opposite, bottom: The glass and steel pavilion seems to float above the arid hillside landscape.

Above: The house is composed of a delicate steel frame, which shelters a glass-enclosed volume perched atop a solid concrete box like a classical temple on its base. The glass box contains a space from which to contemplate the view; the concrete base contains the living areas of the home. Simple square windows open the bedrooms and living areas to the views of the surrounding landscape. The front door, located to the right of the largest window, is barely visible in the concrete wall.

Right: Concept sketch of the house.

Feb. 2000

Campo Baeza's design is certainly abstract and reductivist, but his particular brand of minimalism has an earthy feeling and strong physical presence. The concrete base feels like it is part of the ground, in part because of its rough texture, in part because its color echoes the colors of the dry soil around it. The thin columns and roof slab of the upper pavilion, along with its frameless glass box, are so delicate that they feel almost immaterial. The space they enclose is palpable, not the enclosure itself. It's as if the architect pinned down air and sky atop a concrete box.

Campo Baeza's references are decidedly modern, but not exclusively so. The white color and clean lines of the steel pavilion have strong echoes of Mies van der Rohe's iconic Farnsworth House in Plano, Illinois, one of the defining homes of twentieth century modernism. Like the Farnsworth House, Campo Baeza's structure seems to float above the landscape. The concept of placing an open sanctuary atop a solid plinth is actually quite classical. The analogy of an ancient Roman or Greek temple is apt, given the architect's desire to make a space of quiet contemplation overlooking the rural hillside. This sense of being resolutely modern as well as classical, and of being anchored to the site but floating above it, gives the de Blas house a timeless quality that makes it more about its place than about a particular moment in history.

Above: The glass skin enclosing the viewing platform contains no mullions or frames, so the view outward remains pristine. The glass facade is set back from the steel frame to create a variety of enclosures.

Opposite, top: The lightweight steel structure sits squarely on the concrete roof of the main house. Beyond the glass enclosure is a swimming pool (foreground) that doubles as a reflective water feature.

Opposite, bottom: A narrow staircase leads from the living area on the lower level to the upper level, flooded with light.

Opposite, far right: Top-floor plan (top); ground-floor plan (bottom).

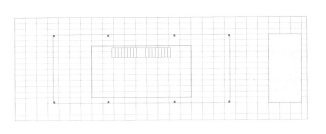

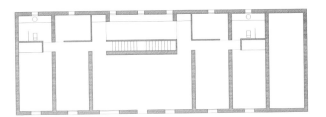

weathering steel house

Shim-Sutcliffe Architects
Toronto, Canada 2002

The unorthodox material cladding the exterior of this
semi-suburban house in Toronto—weathering
Cor-Ten steel—would suggest a heavy, monolithic
structure. But Toronto architects Brigitte Shim and
Howard Sutcliffe made this home for a young family
with two children visually permeable, to lighten the
steel volume's visual weight and fold it subtly into
the landscape.

Located in North York, just a few miles from
downtown Toronto, the house sits at the crest of a wide
wooded ravine, one of several that slice through the
eastern edge of the city. On the street side, the house
takes its place among oversized suburban mansions;
at the rear, the site becomes unexpectedly bucolic as it
opens up to the ravine, with the CN Tower's famous
spire in the distance. Shim and Sutcliffe aligned windows on the front elevation with those on the rear
facade to open up views of the landscape from the
street. But the connection to the landscape involves
more than carefully aligned windows.

On the front of the house, Shim and Sutcliffe
excavated the ground around the children's playroom,
their parents' gym, and service wing to create a
light court that brightens what would otherwise have
remained a dark basement. This carving away of
the ground erodes the monolithic quality of the steel
cladding, as do dining room windows set back into
the facade and a large rain scupper notched into the
steel. As rainwater cascades down the scupper, it
marks the facade with the imprint of time and weather.

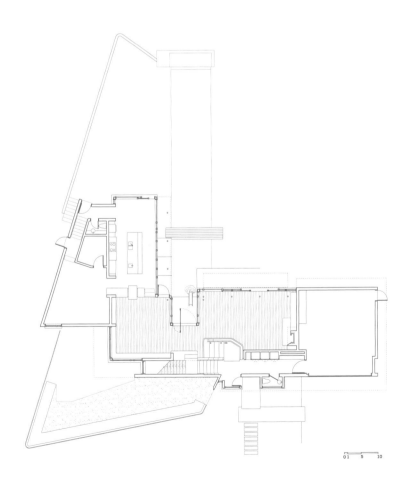

Previous spread: The rear of the house features large windows and sliding glass doors that access a deck and pool.

Top left: The rear facade combines wood, glass, and weathering steel.

Top right: Built-in sunscreens shade the large south-facing windows and glass doors.

Right: Ground-floor plan.

Opposite: The spacious living room boasts nautically inspired detailing of painted steel columns, wood ceilings, and metal handrails.

The rear elevation is much more transparent, opening up the interiors to broad vistas of the wood. In good weather, floor-to-ceiling mahogany-framed windows open up to connect the house physically to the outdoors. During Toronto's long, bitter winters, sun pouring through the large expanses of south-facing glass warms up the interiors. (Overhangs and built-in brise-soleil of wood and steel keep out excess sun in summer.)

The floor plan wraps itself around a small pond with lily pads and a lap pool pointing toward downtown Toronto. Beyond the axial pool is a grove of birch trees that keep the skyline (except for the landmark needle of the CN Tower) veiled in summer. A pivoting glass door in the living room abuts the edge of the water to create an intimate connection between indoors and out.

As in many of their projects, Shim and Sutcliffe wanted daily changes in weather and light to animate their designs. Rainwater pouring down in front of the glass door from a roof scupper into the pond makes a three-dimensional axis of nature. Sunlight reflecting off the pool, which remains heated through the winter to avoid being covered with plastic tarps, casts rippling patterns of light and shadow on the ceilings. In winter, steam rises from the open pool and breathes life into the frozen landscape; in summer, the water seems to flow inside the house, as the owners keep the adjoining glass doors open as much as possible. Over time, the weathering steel has changed the appearance of the entire home: it has mellowed from rusty orange to leathery chocolate brown.

Inside, Shim and Sutcliffe manipulated the floor plan to create up-and-down movement, as if traversing the topography of a natural landscape, a strategy that further ties the architecture to its site. The ground plane steps up from the foyer and mudroom just inside the front door, with a wooden bench built into a wall of Douglas fir storage closets, to the living room and dining room. Beyond is another short staircase down to the kitchen and family room at the very back of the house, which the owners liken to a cozy bear's den. One level up are the master suite, children's rooms, and a guest room. The playroom and gym are one flight down.

Shim and Sutcliffe draw inspiration from far-flung sources: traditional Japanese wooden buildings, Alvar Aalto's Nordic Modernism, and Carlo Scarpa's meticulous modern detailing. But the materials they chose for the house—concrete, painted steel, polished mahogany, Douglas fir, and, of course, weathering steel—are perfectly suited to its unique setting. The house is part of the city yet detached from it, part of the vibrant metropolis as well as the unspoiled Canadian landscape.

Opposite: Glass doors in the living room open onto an axial sequence of water, from a reflecting pool to a lap pool. Beyond the distant trees is the Toronto skyline.

Above: The front corner of the site is cut away to bring light into a basement-level playroom. The front door is located at right, between projecting bays of clear and translucent glass.

Left: The hallway to the second-floor bedrooms receives daylight from various windows.

Above: In winter, the house creates a warm, richly colored counterpoint to the snow-covered landscape.

Left: Site plan.

Opposite: The architects designed the water features so they don't require pool covers in winter, allowing the water to become a year-round element.

tubac house

Rick Joy Architects
Tubac, Arizona, United States 2001

Tucson architect Rick Joy is best known for his work with rammed earth, a sustainable building technique in which soil mixed with cement is tamped down, like poured concrete, to create richly layered walls of stratified earth. Aside from its similarity to adobe, a staple of construction in the American Southwest, rammed earth has an obvious resonance with the region: It is literally made from its site.

In a house he designed in Tubac, fifty miles south of Tucson and as many miles north of the Mexican border, Joy looked to Cor-Ten steel instead of rammed earth. Weathering steel, a tough material for a house, brings a different understanding of site to a house located among the reddish-brown hills of the Sonoran Desert. It harmonizes with the colors of the place; it also picks up on the Southwestern vernacular of rusty metal silos and sheds.

Joy designed the house for a retired couple from Ohio as two separate sheds bermed into a desert hillside. The smaller volume, measuring 1,500 square feet (139 square meters), contains a garage, workshop, and two guest bedrooms. The angular shed roofs recall the profile of the surrounding mountains, while the low-slung massing purposely keeps the house close to the ground so as not to dominate the mostly flat, arid site. The larger volume, covering 2,500 square feet (232 square meters), contains a loft-like living/dining room, kitchen, master suite, separate offices for the husband and wife, and a large covered porch overlooking a swimming pool. The blocks are skewed from each other to face slightly different views of the mountains. Between them is a wedge-shaped concrete staircase that leads down from the driveway and entry path at the top of the hill into a surprisingly urbane courtyard with cubic fountains and planted trees and succulents. Joy conceived of the pinched staircase between the wings of the house as a canyon that descends from the hot, arid plain into a cool, shady oasis. The view as one descends the staircase is one of the clients' favorite vistas of the Tumacacori Mountains.

Joy clad the exterior in large sheets of Cor-Ten steel and capped it with a corrugated metal roof. He left both materials unsealed so they would quickly weather to a rusty copper color that picks up the palette of the surrounding landscape of snow-capped desert mountains and wild mesquite trees. The rusty exteriors recall the ersatz silos and sheds of the Arizona desert as well as the rugged, muscular sculptures of Richard Serra, especially given the home's stark angular forms. It's a fitting reference point for the clients, who are avid fans of contemporary art and architecture.

Inside, polished materials in a cool neutral palette contrast with the aggressive exterior. Joy selected waxed concrete floors, maple cabinetry, a stainless steel kitchen, plaster walls, and a combination of clear

and translucent glass that modulates views and light throughout the house. Classic modernist furniture makes it clear that this is a sophisticated work of contemporary architecture, not a rustic desert folly.

The open views from the house appeal to the clients' interest in astronomy: Both enjoy stargazing and watching lightning storms march across the desert. Joy gave them large expanses of mullionless glass, shaded from the sun by deep overhangs, which open entire rooms to the views and bring the outdoors in. Joy also provided smaller, more focused vistas with strategically placed window openings that frame specific elements in the landscape like vivid full-color photographs. The careful placement of windows also helps draw hot air up and out by creating a venturi, or chimney effect.

Previous spread: An outdoor room shaded by a deep, sloping roof overhang steps down to a pool. Surrounding the house are the peaks of the desert mountains of Tubac, Arizona.

Opposite: Seen from the entry drive, the two volumes comprising the house appear to be buried into the arid hillside. A deep roof overhang shades a large expanse of glass on the structure containing the workshop and guest rooms.

Above: Built-in planters with desert trees give the entry courtyard a sophisticated, almost urban air. At left is the main house, clad in rusty steel.

Left: The living/dining area is an open loft-like space with large windows framing views of the desert landscape.

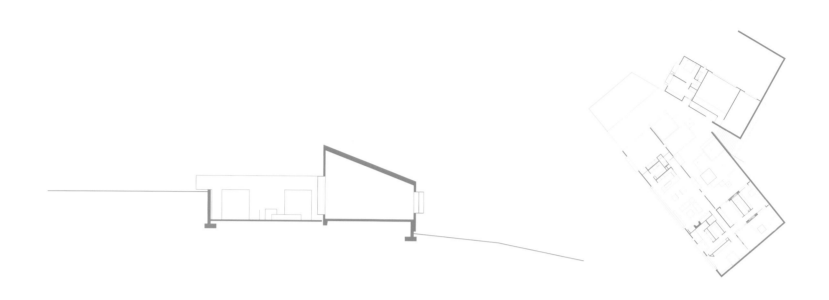

Opposite, top: Section (left); floor plan (right).

Opposite, left: The profile of the home's two wings echos the mountain ranges in the distance. At left is the volume containing the workshop, garage, and guest rooms; at right is the main house.

Opposite, top right: The Cor-Ten steel cladding recalls the rusty metal sheds and silos common throughout the American Southwest.

Opposite, bottom right: A small window with a deep surround takes on a sculptural quality reminiscent of works by Donald Judd, while keeping out the strong desert sun.

Above: The play between the low-slung volumes of the main house and the excavated hillside site creates unexpected courtyards.

Outdoor living has been a central idea in Arizona's desert modernism since the time of Frank Lloyd Wright. Joy gave his clients the equivalent of an outdoor living room, a great open-air porch adjoining the black granite swimming pool at the edge of a terrace. The deep overhang of the rusty steel roof creates a shady space for relaxing or entertaining, supported by an outdoor kitchen with built-in barbeque. A large cutout gives the effect of a giant window in the side wall of a room open to the elements.

Joy's design draws inspiration from its desert setting in many ways: materials, massing, and spaces. The way it brings the outside in and opens the interiors to the landscape and climate are among its most important contributions to the tradition of desert modernism.

The large Copenhagen firm Henning Larsens Tegnestue designed this small, sublime summer home and studio for a gallery owner. More than a house, the structure is a simple wooden pavilion nestled in a lush fern grove in Vejby Strand, on Denmark's northern Zeeland coast. The single volume covers just 100 square meters (328 square feet), but provides a variety of spatial arrangements.

At the center of the box-like building is a brick core containing a bathroom and kitchen separated by two fireplaces. Wood pocket doors slide out of the core to create four distinct spaces within the open volume: a studio, living area, porch, and kitchen. Or, when the doors are left open, the interior becomes a single light-filled loft in the woods.

The architects set the house in a clearing in the fern-covered woods. The pavilion's east and north exterior walls are clad in larch siding, with a full-height glass wall on the south elevation that brings the outdoors in; a wood-framed glass door at the eastern edge of the glazed wall opens onto a small wood terrace. The entry is from a larger wooden terrace on the western side of the house. This west elevation features large glass doors screened by large expanses of wooden slats, which can be hinged up and fixed horizontally like awnings.

The architects clad the interiors in birch plywood panels. The materials are inexpensive but exactingly detailed; they take on a more dramatic feeling when sunlight through the slatted western wall fills the space with patterns of light and shadow. In contrast to the completely glazed south facade, the north wall has only a narrow strip of glass along the floor. Instead of an open expanse of woodland scenery, the view is a sliver of the forest floor. However, the cool northern light reflecting against the polished wood floor bounces soft daylight into the studio—where the owner can focus on his artistic endeavors rather than be distracted by the lush panorama of the landscape outside. A strip of skylight at the back of the space also brings a soft wash of northern light, artists' preferred source of daylight, into the studio.

The precise detailing of the larch exterior and birch interior gives the house a decidedly Scandinavian feeling—an abstract, modern interpretation of a Danish country house. It also has a Japanese air—especially the studio, whose wood-sheathed walls and ceiling have a gridded geometric pattern not unlike the modular tatami mats of traditional Japanese interiors.

Although Henning Larsens Tegnestue's design interprets Danish tradition in contemporary language, it is also part of a strong modernist tradition of crafting small, precisely engineered gems. Perhaps the most famous is the Cabanon, or cabin, that Le Corbusier built in Cap Martin on the French Riviera in 1952. Corbusier's tiny seaside hut—just 16 square meters, or 172 square feet—is not the grand design statement one might expect from one of the founding fathers of twentieth-century modernism. It is a house that boils down the needs of a quiet retreat to its bare essentials. Nothing is extraneous, yet it provided its owner with everything he needed. Larsens Tegnestue's contemporary cabin removes every distraction to create a sophisticated retreat in the woods.

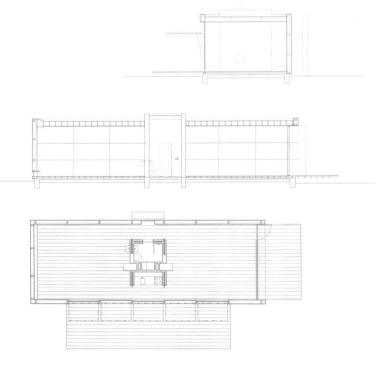

Previous spread: The wood cabin structure appears to float above the fern-covered ground of the densely wooded site.

Opposite, top: The west facade features slatted wooden screens over large sliding glass doors. The screens can be propped open to create fixed awnings.

Opposite, bottom: Cross section (top); longitudinal section (center); plan (bottom).

Above: The studio space brings in soft northern light through a narrow skylight and a floor-level band of glass.

Right: Wood pocket doors slide out of the central core to partition off smaller spaces within the single-room structure.

koehler house

Julie Snow Architects
New Brunswick, Canada 2000

The coast of New Brunswick in eastern Canada is blessed with a dramatic coastline of craggy granite cliffs studded with spruce and pine trees. But this place of tremendous natural beauty is also one of great danger. Aside from the epic coastal storms called Nor'easters that spin up the Atlantic Coast in winter, bringing howling winds and heavy snow, the area has some of the highest and quickest-moving tides in the world. The water levels in some spots along the Fundy coast can rise four to eight feet per hour during high tide.

Architect Julie Snow designed a hilltop vacation house on 55 acres overlooking the Bay of Fundy that tempers an incredible openness and transparency—to enjoy spectacular seaside views from every room—with safeguards against the site's rough, tempestuous climate. Both the architect and her clients are from Minneapolis, which guaranteed that the house would be properly designed for the harshest winter weather, even though it was meant primarily as a summer retreat. The two-story home has a simple parti: two horizontal planes anchored to a rocky outcropping and shifted slightly against each other to create long outdoor decks that reach out into the landscape. At 140 square meters (1,500 square feet), the house is not grand, but its huge expanses of glass with lightweight frames make it feel much larger. Snow uses the borrowed view technique of Japanese landscape painting, where the distant vista is treated as an extension of interior space to expand the apparent size of the indoor space. Aside from creating the illusion of added space, wrapping the house almost entirely in glass ensures that the dramatic granite cliff and uninterrupted view of the open sea are visible from every room in the house.

One enters the house on the lower level and passes through a small foyer to reach an open living/dining area and kitchen. To the right of the double-height living space is a guest bedroom and bath, cozily buried into the rocky hillside; to the left, beyond the dining area, is a screened-in covered porch. Upstairs is a sitting room and master suite with a private screened porch. On the opposite side of the house, reached by a catwalk overlooking the double-height living area, is a long, open terrace that points toward the open sea like the prow of a streamlined modern ship.

Snow tied the overlapping platforms to a stone volume anchored into the rocky cliff, which contains a fireplace, heating equipment, and storage. The strategy takes clues from Frank Lloyd Wright's iconic Fallingwater near Pittsburgh, Pennsylvania, one of the most famous of twentieth-century houses. Wright anchored what he considered to be the heart of the home—the hearth—into a rock formation alongside a waterfall, from which he daringly cantilevered rooms

Previous spread: The house
commands a dramatic rocky cliff
overlooking the sea, but
still manages to blend in with its
stark surroundings.

Opposite: The house floats
above the rocky landscape,
supported on shallow piers.

Above left: The house steps
down as the cliff slopes down to
the water.

Above right: The stone wall containing the fireplace anchors the
house to its site.

and terraces out into the landscape. Snow took a similar approach: The solid fireplace wall, clad in bluestone, creates visual and structural ballast for what appears to be a delicate glass structure perched perilously above the beautiful but dangerous coastline.

The interior is casual and completely open, like a seaside loft. The architect kept spaces as open as possible. For instance, she designed the kitchen as two low islands floating between the living and dining areas to maintain unobstructed views from both spaces. Appliances and storage are all tucked beneath the counters. The expertly crafted interiors have a nautical air, though not with obvious ship-building details: hardwood floors, maple paneling, and translucent metal fabric stretched across the balustrade of the second-floor catwalk. The rest of the material palette of Douglas fir columns, bluestone walls, and

glass, is barely perceptible, so that the sea and the sky become the dominant elements.

The downside of such an open, permeable home is that it can leave its occupants feeling vulnerable in gale-force winds and blinding storms. Snow responded by adding sliding wood panels that can be drawn across the bedroom window walls. They create a sense of shelter when it's forbidding outside in winter, and also cut down on excessive sun in summer. With such thoughtful details, Snow ensured a house that can be enjoyed year-round, and one that celebrates—as much as it respects—its powerful site in every kind of weather.

Opposite: The glass exterior
opens up views from
every room of the house.

Top left: A dramatic ocean
view appears at the top of
the stairs.

Top right: A stone-clad core
anchors the steel-framed house.

Left: The open kitchen in the
dramatic double-height
main living space features low
counters that don't interrupt
the view.

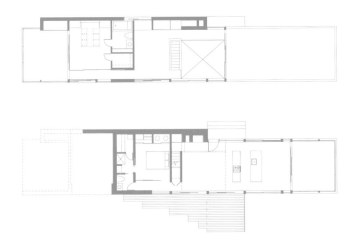

Opposite: A stepped wooden deck off the living/dining room creates a spot from which to enjoy the dramatic view.

Above: At night, the glass house glows like a lantern in the landscape.

Left: Second-floor plan (top); ground-floor plan (bottom);

casa equis

Barclay & Crousse Architecture
Cañete, Peru 2003

Paris-based architects Sandra Barclay and Jean-Pierre Crousse designed three houses at La Escondida, an enclave of beach retreats near the town of Cañete, Peru, about 85 miles south of Lima. All three respond to their setting on a crescent of precipitously steep, sandy cliffs overlooking the Pacific. The latest, Casa Equis, takes the architects' ideas of merging architecture and landscape and indoor and outdoor space to their most sophisticated resolution.

Cañete is located in the Atacama Desert of Southern Peru and Northern Chile, one of the most arid regions on earth. The landscape is so completely barren and scaleless that it challenges all conventions of building in the desert. There is hardly any vegetation at all; the desert hills are so uniform in color and texture that virtually any structure built on them stands out as a man-made object. It is, as Jean-Pierre Crousse says, an absolute void. The benefit of such a harsh climate, however, is that rain is virtually unknown and humidity nonexistent, so outdoor living is remarkably easy and comfortable. The most important demands on architects building there are to provide adequate shade from the strong tropical sun and to ensure that structures are seismically stable in the event of an earthquake.

Barclay and Crousse decided that abstraction was the best way to mitigate the vast scale of the desert. They looked to native Peruvian textile patterns and the nearby pre-Inca ruins of Pachacamac, a hillside city dating from 200 B.C., for inspiration. They carved the spaces of Casa Equis from the steep hillside and kept its exteriors as neutral as possible to keep the house from standing out as an object on the fragile landscape. Barclay suggests that the subtle palette of reddish-brown local stone and concrete painted ochre or left raw makes the architecture look

Previous spread: A mesh
canopy shades an open deck of
the living/dining room
with views of the Pacific Ocean.

Opposite, top: The swimming
pool defines the edge
of the top-floor terrace. Behind
is a neighboring house
also designed by Barclay
and Crousse.

Opposite, bottom: The home's
stepped volumes and
earth-tone exterior echo the
surrounding cliffs.

Above left: An exterior
staircase leads to the lower-
level bedrooms.

Above right: The glass-enclosed
edge of the swimming pool
extends dramatically over the
outdoor staircase.

Right: Exploded axonometric of
top floor (left) and bottom floor
(right).

as if it has always been there. The open-air hallways and living spaces draw inspiration from the open courtyards of the late-nineteenth and early twentieth century ranchos. These Neoclassical summer homes, largely abandoned after a devastating earthquake in the 1940s, extend for miles along the seaside cliffs south of Lima. But whereas the ranchos were formal and axial, the spaces of Casa Equis are decidedly modern. Space flows fluidly from one room to another, from inside to outside.

When arriving by car, one parks and enters the two-story, 1,800-square-foot (167.2-square-meter) house at the uppermost level. The entry is through a wood-planked courtyard with a concrete roof volume that frames a dramatic view of the Pacific Ocean. The top floor contains the kitchen, service courtyard, living and dining rooms, and a terrace extending to a lap pool at its edge, overlooking the sea. A long concrete stair leads from the entry courtyard down to two children's rooms with double sets of bunk beds, a guest

Opposite: Sliding glass doors in a lower-level bedroom open onto views of the beach. A built-in concrete bench doubles as a balustrade.

Above: A brightly colored wall spans the space between the indoors (with fireplace at right) and outdoors.

Left: Sliding glass panels retract to completely open the living/dining room to the outdoors.

Opposite, top: The thick concrete encasing the swimming pool defines a shady balcony off the master bedroom.

Opposite, bottom left: Longitudinal section (top); cross-section (bottom).

Opposite, bottom right: An open-air corridor opens onto a lower-level guest bedroom.

Above: A terrace off the master bedroom, shaded by the underside of the swimming pool above, opens onto views of the ocean.

room with an oceanfront terrace, and the master suite, also with a private terrace overlooking the ocean. Separating the children's and adult's bedrooms is a grotto-like open-air vestibule crowned by the wood slats of the terrace above. Sun streams down between the planks, creating stripes of light on the concrete floor, which is mixed with rough pebble aggregate.

The connections between inside and out are many. Barclay and Crousse eliminated doors and walls as much as possible, keeping circulation open to the elements. A wall of sliding glass doors between the living/dining room and the large top-floor terrace completely erases boundaries between indoor and outdoor space; the flow from inside to outside is seamless, with a rose-colored concrete wall providing continuity between the two areas. Gauzy tennis-court mesh creates a breezy, inexpensive awning to shade what the architects call an "artificial beach," a terrace framed by the lap pool and the sea beyond.

The architects strategically framed views of the ocean and the dry, rocky cliffs, further connecting architecture and landscape and interior and exterior space. Deep overhangs create shade and capture a patch of sea and sky. The most dramatic is the view from the entry court down the concrete stairs. As one descends to the bedroom level, the cantilevered lap pool enclosed in solid glass creates a deep cobalt edge against the blue of the sea and sky. As Crousse suggests, the home's framing of dramatic views makes the views even better. And its intimate connections between inside and out make being outside even more delightful.

mountain tree guest house

Mack Scogin Merrill Elam Architects
Dillard, Georgia, United States 2001

About 80 miles north of Atlanta, deep in the Appalachian woodlands that straddle the North Carolina border, is the tiny hamlet of Dillard, Georgia. In 1996, architects Mack Scogin and Merrill Elam designed a rural retreat for an Atlanta couple on 24 wooded acres here. Several years later, the clients called again and asked the architects to create a small addition to their property to accommodate their growing family. They needed a guest suite with added privacy and a garage with storage space for an automobile as well as tools and gardening equipment.

Scogin and Elam responded with a 186-square-meter (2,000-square-foot) mini-compound just uphill from the existing house. The secluded, self-contained addition includes a garage, bedroom suite, and a long cantilevered deck that extends into the dense woods like a pier jutting out to the sea. Although its striking rectilinear design is decidedly not a part of the natural landscape, the architects took great care to create a structure that would strike a harmonious relationship with its natural surroundings. To wit, a stand of live bamboo planted beneath the deck grows up through a slot cut into the slate-covered platform, firmly tying the terrace to its site. Vertical gaps between Cor-Ten panels surrounding the unusual deck create slits of light along the steel enclosure, like shafts of sunlight piercing the forest canopy. The steel columns beneath the deck blend perfectly with the tall trees around them. In fact, the columns seem to disappear into the woods like more towering trunks, adding to the vertical rhythm of the forest.

The integration of the house into the landscape begins with its position on the hillside. The garage is on grade, but to reach the bedroom, bathroom, and terrace above, one ascends a concrete ramp that rises along a concrete retaining wall. As it nears the upper level, the ramp is sandwiched between the solid back wall of the bedroom and a layer of translucent glass. The path has an upward thrust that plays against the energy created by the bedroom cantilevering over the garage and the terrace darting into the woods.

The materials have an unpolished quality that seems appropriate for the rustic setting. The garage is built of poured-in-place concrete with a band of windows in the upper reaches of the concrete wall. Like the edging of the long terrace, the deep roof overhang above the small, boxy bedroom structure is wrapped in rusty Cor-Ten steel. The front and side walls of the bedroom are floor-to-ceiling panes of clear and translucent glass, which have an extraordinary effect of anchoring the space to its setting. From inside, the glass skin is almost completely uninterrupted; only thin vertical mullions break up the glazed expanses. From outside, the glass, which extends flush with the Cor-Ten underside of the cantilevered structure, takes on the reflection of the woods around it. Scogin and

Previous spread: The long
walkway, supported on slender
columns, echoes the rhythm
of tree trunks in the woods. The
main guest house structure
is at left.

Opposite, top left: The glass-
enclosed bedroom cantilevers
over the driveway.

Opposite, top right: Slate flooring from the inside extends
onto the terrace. A stand of
bamboo grows up through a
grate in the deck.

Opposite, bottom left:
Elevations.

Opposite, bottom right: A
ramped walkway passes
between the bedroom, at left,
and a wall of translucent glass.

Above: At dusk, the glass-
enclosed bedroom pavilion
seems to float above its clearing
in the woods.

Elam brought the outside indoors, and reflected the
outdoors on the exterior surface. The way in which the
exterior blends into the landscape is a sophisticated
architectural sleight-of-hand.

At every turn, the house confounds the separation between indoor and outdoor space. Scogin and
Elam consider the terrace an extension of the interior,
an idea reinforced by the continuation of the slate
flooring onto the outside deck. The blurring of boundaries also erodes distinctions between architectural
features and the surrounding forest. The ramp,
for instance, is artificial, but feels like a natural trail up
the hillside; walking along the terrace is akin to a walk
through the trees. Scogin and Elam's design is a harmonious blending of the manmade and natural worlds.

picture window house

Shigeru Ban Architects
Izu, Shizuoka, Japan 2002

In space-starved Japan, it's difficult to find open views of sea and sky, even outside the country's crowded cities. On the Izu Peninsula, 60 miles south of Tokyo, architect Shigeru Ban designed a house that takes full advantage of a rare commodity anywhere in Japan, and especially so close to Tokyo: an isolated hillside site with few neighbors in sight and an uninterrupted view of the Pacific Ocean. Ban took the idea of opening the house up to the view with large windows one step further. He made the entire house a large window framing the views—hence the name, the Picture Window House.

Ban first gained fame for his inventive structures built with cardboard tubes. Other projects, such as the Curtain Wall House in Tokyo (1995), demonstrated his tongue-in-cheek approach to serious explorations of liberating open spaces to capture the freedom of contemporary urban life. In that project, Ban played on the idea of a curtain wall by wrapping the home's top two floors in a billowy fabric curtain that can be drawn open to expose the private home to the public realm. With the curtains open or closed, the house is a jaw-dropping sight in the middle of Tokyo. Ban's work also interprets traditional Japanese shoji screens in a more contemporary language. Other houses look to sliding panels and moveable partitions to create open, flexible interiors.

The Picture Window House is as dramatic as the Curtain Wall House, but more restrained. The 274-square-meter (2,950-square-foot) structure sits atop a steep slope overlooking the Pacific. The plan of the two-story house is exceedingly simple: a long rectangular bar. Its arrangement of spaces, however, is eccentric.

The entry-level ground floor is a huge open volume with a living/dining room and kitchen. Large 8-foot-square glass doors on both of the long elevations slide open on tracks to create a giant semi-outdoor space. A deep overhanging roof on the south-facing oceanfront elevation keeps the sun out. Upstairs is a double-height studio at one end of the long bar and a storage area at the other. In between are four bedrooms placed in a row, with floor-to-ceiling windows overlooking the sea. Behind the bedrooms, along the north end of the structure, is an unusually long bathroom that also acts as the hallway to the sleeping quarters. The bathroom suite-cum-hallway, where the main staircase from the ground floor arrives, contains one bathtub, two toilets, and five sinks; only glass walls and doors separate the three areas within the bathroom, one with a sink, tub, and toilet, a second, larger space with three sinks, and the third with a toilet and sink. Clearly, privacy is not a top priority for this family.

The material palette is minimal and sleek, primarily painted steel and lots of glass. (Adjustable aluminum louvers on the second-floor exterior, accentuating the horizontal lines of the house, can be retracted to create a completely transparent facade.) The steel structure functions like a bridge, with the braced two-story spaces on either end anchoring the huge column-free span of the bedrooms over the living area. Diagonal braces are visible through the bedroom windows.

Many modern architects try to integrate indoor and outdoor space, but few succeed with as much aplomb as Ban. The open living room of the Picture Window house is dramatic even when its glass facades are closed, with long, clean views of the wooded slope along one side and of the ocean on the other. When they are open, however, the doors stack neatly on opposite ends of the house, removing all traces of enclosure. Only the metal tracks concealed discretely in the floor and ceiling give any clues that the interior can be closed off from the elements. The resulting 20-meter-long (66-foot-long) opening is sublime. The extension of the wood floor out to the terrace reinforces the notion that the room is a seamless flow of space from inside to outside.

The elegant system of sliding doors is clearly Ban's nod to the delicate shoji screens of traditional Japanese architecture. Beyond tying the Picture Window House into his country's architectural traditions, the minimal enclosure anchors the house to its site, making the most of its quiet setting.

Previous spread: Large glass doors on the oceanfront facade slide to opposite sides of the house to create a completely open living space on the ground floor.

Above: Exposed diagonal braces in the bedrooms create a huge truss that allows the ground floor to remain free of columns.

Opposite, top: When large glass doors slide open, the living area extends out to a deck with a view of the ocean.

Opposite, bottom: Ground-floor plan (top); second-floor plan (bottom); Exploded axonometric (right).

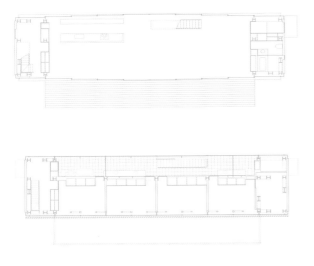

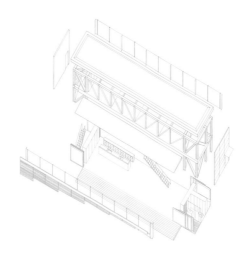

Opposite, top: The column-free
ground floor space creates an
uninterrupted view of the sea.
A staircase at left leads up to the
second-floor bedrooms and
bathroom.

Opposite, bottom: A glass-
enclosed bathroom extending
the length of the second floor
doubles as a hallway to reach the
bedrooms, located behind the
bathroom.

Above: A glass-enclosed hall-
way-cum-bathroom on the
second floor appears to float
above the open ground floor.

Right: Cross-section.

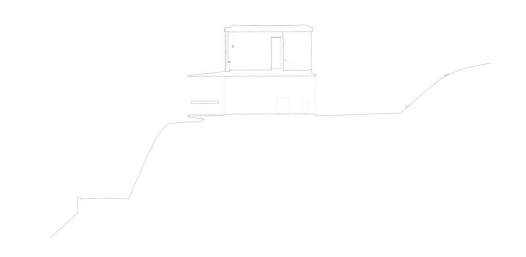

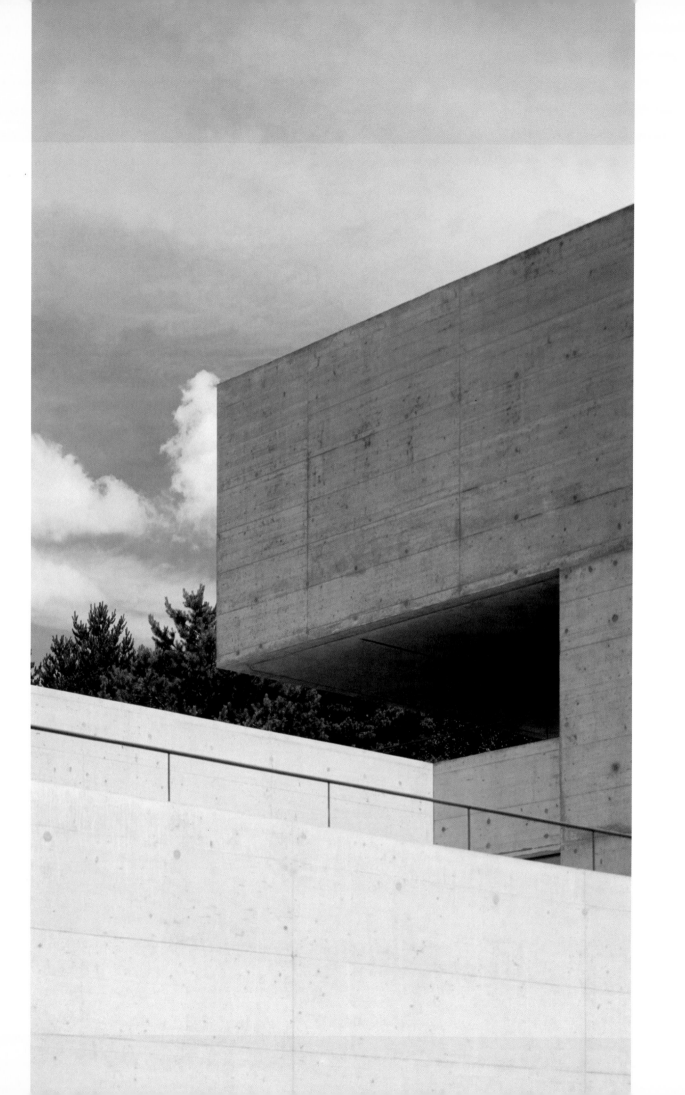

02 reimagining the program

The way people live is changing at breakneck speed, but the houses most people live in have changed little over the generations. The traditional housing types that still populate most of the developed world haven't progressed much in centuries. They reflect a family structure that almost universally consisted of a married couple with children, where the father (and only the father) went to work outside the home. These days, the size and structure of families varies greatly, as do the activities that take place in the home. The divisions between work and rest are becoming harder to distinguish, as more members of the workforce choose to—or must—work from home. People are living longer, which often means sharing space with grown children and grandchildren under the same roof. And as lives become more complicated and stressful, there is a greater emphasis on time and space for leisure, whether screening rooms and home gyms or second homes where people can escape the pressures of the workweek. The houses in this section reflect clever solutions to the kinds of changes clients are seeking in their lives.

Technology has greatly eroded the need for a proper workplace distinct from the home. In the last decade alone, laptops, cellular phones, PDAs, and wireless Internet have made working from home easier and less expensive. The house is no longer a refuge one leaves in the morning and comes home to in the evening after a long day at the office; for millions, home is the workplace. Those who have made a long-term commitment to working at home or who have full-fledged businesses with employees and visiting clients can't easily work from a den or a spare bedroom. Many choose to create a work environment that is distinct from domestic areas but somehow integrated with the rest of the house. Others want a home where work and leisure are completely intertwined. For instance, the graphic designers who commissioned Toyo Ito to design a live/work house in Tokyo (page 98) wanted a fluid house with few separations between spaces for working, sleeping, eating, or, when possible, relaxing. Ito decided to create flexible spaces that could be used for work or play.

For those who spend tiring workweeks in the city—whether at home or in a traditional office—a weekend house in the country is becoming more a necessity for mental well-being than a luxury item. A second home where one can escape is not the status object it used to be. Accordingly, architects are helping clients develop affordable getaways that suit the kind of low-key lifestyles they want to lead on weekends. Architect Drew Heath designed a tiny but well-conceived cabin in the Australian brush for a busy couple from Sydney (page 88). The one-room, 25-square-meter (269-square-foot) house is more like an architectonic tent, with space for sleeping, storage, and little else. There is no indoor plumbing or kitchen, but the cabin gives the clients the bare essentials for enjoying peace and quiet. And at a cost of just US $20,000, the cabin gets to the core of what is truly necessary in a second home.

The vacation compound designed by Toshiko Mori on the Gulf Coast of Florida (page 142) is a far more polished, sophisticated structure. But the project still tackles the issue of how people want to live in their second homes. Mori opted for a soaring, loft-like interior without strict separation of functions and spaces. The idea of an open, unprogrammed home makes sense: Who wants a structured vacation house when they seek relaxing, unstructured activities? Beyond the main house, Mori ensured that the guest house and pool structure had privacy, placing each within a separate precinct carved out of the tropical landscape.

Balancing privacy with shared public space remains an important consideration in the home, especially when large families or multiple generations live together. Architects are solving this dilemma in innovative ways. The C House in Tokyo by Kei'ichi Irie (page 104) is one of the more extreme examples of a house that balances the privacy requirements of a large family with their need for shared space. The architect had to squeeze quarters for a married couple, their young children, and an elderly parent into a small city lot in the middle of Tokyo. Irie decided to give the parents maximum privacy with a master suite that literally detaches itself from the rest of the house with a small bridge over a double-height open space, and put the grandmother's bedroom downstairs near the children's, but separated by a bathroom suite. On the flip side, Irie celebrates the coming together of the family during shared mealtimes with a built-in glass table that stretches most of the length of the living area. The table maintains a constant height even though the floor beneath it rises up several steps; as a result, a single surface acts as kitchen counter, Western-style dining table, and Japanese-style dining table with seating on the floor.

Other architects follow similar strategies of giving breathing space to large families. In Liechtenstein, Baumschlager–Eberle's stark concrete Flatz House (page 156) puts children's bedrooms in a separate volume cantilevered dramatically above the master suite, creating a shady and very private terrace off the parents' bedroom. Will Bruder designed a large compound on the Massachusetts coast (page 134) with a horizontal separation of wings for children and adults. The fluid, organically shaped house gives the children their own wing, with bedrooms, bathrooms, and entertainment spaces far removed from the master wing at the opposite end.

For many architects, the solution to so many conflicting needs is to design highly flexible homes, with floor plans that can adapt to growing children, shrinking families, and rooms that can handle multiple functions. Adaptability is what will distinguish the home of the future from the still-present houses of the past.

Opposite: The Flatz House in Liechtenstein, designed by Baumschlager–Eberle, separates children's and parent's bedrooms.

Top: Gary Chang designed the Suitcase House for maximum flexibility, with minimal, mobile furniture and floor hatches opening to subterranean sleeping quarters.

Above: Toshiko Mori's compound on the Florida coast features a freestanding guest cottage for added privacy.

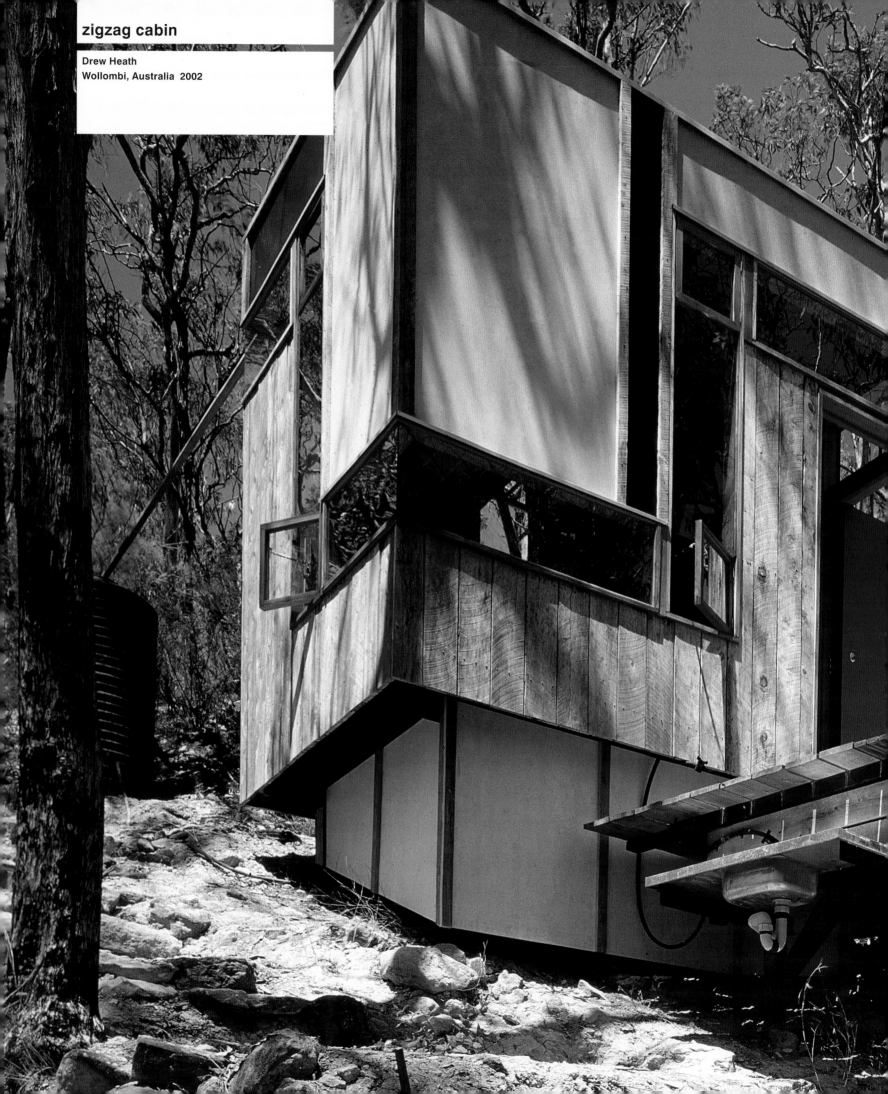

zigzag cabin

Drew Heath
Wollombi, Australia 2002

This weekend cabin designed by Sydney architect and builder Drew Heath for a city-dwelling couple is remarkable for its small size and equally small budget. The house covers less than 25 square meters (269 square feet) and was built for only US $20,000. Despite—or perhaps because of—such constraints, with minimal means Heath created an exciting, energetic work of architecture that maximizes the very inspiration for a busy urban couple from Sydney to build a second home. The cabin has all of the essentials needed to enjoy the peace and quiet of its natural surroundings, but few extra frills. It is more like a camp tent than a proper cabin or cottage, but it allows the clients to escape the city and relax just the same.

The Zigzag Cabin, so named because of the pattern of narrow strip windows slicing across its facades, sits on a steep hillside surrounded by eucalyptus forest in Wollombi, a few hours' drive north of Sydney. The structure rises above the steep slope on pilings. Two wooden decks extend downhill from the house to create outdoor living space and viewing platforms from which to enjoy the landscape, always in an informal manner.

The box-like structure contains just 9 square meters (97 square feet) of space; there is room for two built-in beds on the ground floor, with a staircase leading up to an additional bunk on a tiny mezzanine level. Storage for everything needed for a weekend in the country fits into built-in storage beneath the beds: cooking equipment, hammocks, and lanterns. (The analogy to a campsite tent applies to the compact size of the house, as well as to the bare-bones amenities.) There is no indoor plumbing. The sink is located at the edge of the deck platform, fed with rainwater collected in a tank uphill behind the cabin. With so little interior space, the owners spend most of their time on the outdoor deck, weather permitting. Unless besieged by rains, there is every incentive to spend as much time outdoors as possible.

Structurally, the box-like cabin is indeed a box, with a wood frame tied together at the parapet level. Heath designed the structural framing so that the narrow wood windows could wind their way up and across the facades, with operable square panels

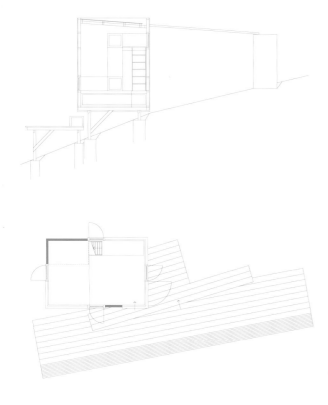

Previous spread: The only plumbing is an outdoor sink at the edge of the deck, which is fed by a water tank located uphill from the cabin.

Top left: The tiny weekend cabin, covering just 25 square meters, sits along a deck extending from a remote hillside in Australia.

Top right: Equipment for an entire weekend visit fits into built-in storage cubbies beneath the two beds. A ladder leads up to an extra sleeping berth.

Left: Cross section (top); floor plan (bottom).

Above: Operable square windows are located at the crossing—the zigzag—between vertical and horizontal strips of glass in the wood facade.

Opposite: Low horizontal strips of glass set into the simple wood skin open up views of the forest from the built-in beds.

inserted at the crossings between horizontal and vertical bands of glass. He clad the structure in inexpensive masonite and rough cypress pine siding that lets the cabin blend in with the scaly texture and silvery skin of the surrounding eucalyptus forest.

Heath's great interest is in designing sustainable buildings that impact the land minimally. His hands-on approach to building his own designs makes him keenly aware of the nature of materials he uses. The Zigzag Cabin is exceedingly simple—so simple, in fact, that the architect was able to secure the necessary building approvals in less than a month. But it gives the clients exactly what they wanted while intruding in the most minimal way on its delicate, arid site.

alonso-planas house

Carlos Ferrater and Joan Guibernau
Barcelona, Spain 1998

Barcelona architects Carlos Ferrater and Joan Guibernau designed this house for multiple generations of a single family. The house sits high up on a trapezoidal-shaped site cut into the slope of a mountain located above a residential area southwest of the city. The architects oriented the volumes perpendicular to the site's topographical contour lines to maximize its commanding views of Barcelona and the Llobregat plain from its hilltop setting.

The house covers 886 square meters (9,533 square feet) spread throughout several interconnected volumes comprising the main living quarters, a garage, and a studio. (One of the owners is a painter; the other, a sculptor.) The house sits at the highest point of the site, which rises 16 meters (52 feet) from the bottom of the curving driveway leading up to the garage. As one winds up the drive, the house seems to tower over the site with a stern, minimalist language of sharp lines and bold massing.

The architects wanted to give the family autonomy in their particular areas of the house, but also wanted to create overlaps and connections between spaces. For instance, they cut a large circular skylight into a concrete terrace and viewing platform that lets light into the entrance to the garage below. The circular cutout also creates an interrelationship between inside and outside, between an outward-looking space (the terrace) and a more introverted space (the garage). The spacious studio is buried into the hillside; only a long row of angled skylights peeking out above the ground is visible from outside. The angled line of skylights defines one of the edges for the broad, flat expanse of lawn and a large swimming pool adjoining the house. The other boundaries of this outdoor "room" are two retaining walls and the louvered facade of the house itself.

Ferrater and Guibernau extended the same dark quartzite stone used inside as the flooring to the patio and pool deck outside. In fact, the floor extends seamlessly from the interior to the terrace to the very edge of the pool, all located on the same level.

Ferrater counts the great expressionistic architect and sculptor Antonio Gaudí, a fellow Catalan, as an important influence, especially Gaudí's fascination with how light penetrates dark underground spaces. Ferrater also cites the work of more thoroughly modern architects who created striking, sometimes unsettling plays of abstraction: Giuseppe Terragni and other Italian rationalists, the Brazilian modernist Lina Bo Bardi, José Luis Sert, and, more recently, Álvaro Siza. The Alonso-Planas house clearly reveals Ferrater's interest in an architecture of abstraction and strong, large-scale moves.

The wood-framed windows on the main living areas' south- and west-facing facades are screened with wide aluminum louvers painted white. The large scale of the louvers plays proportional tricks on one's perception of their dimensions: They appear to be grossly exaggerated in size, which gives the house an even stronger presence on the landscape and a grander scale inside. For all of the home's abstraction, however, its use of natural materials and the interplays of natural light give it a comforting natural edge.

Previous spread: As seen from
the driveway leading up to the
house, painted aluminum louvers on two facades confound
the home's sense of scale.

Opposite, left: Strong shapes
and abstract textures dominate
the exterior of the home.

Opposite, right: The swimming
pool is sheltered behind tall
walls.

Above: Overscaled aluminum
louvers dominate the elevation
facing the entry drive.

Left: Dark quartzite stone used
as interior flooring extends out
to a terrace along the pool.

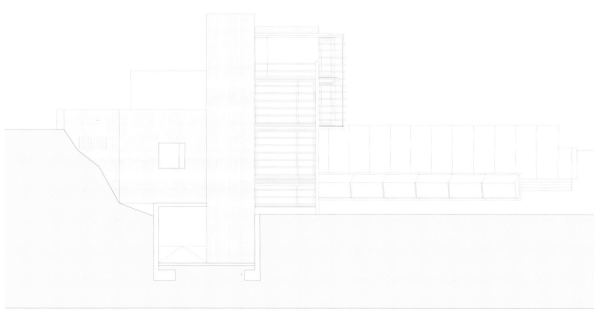

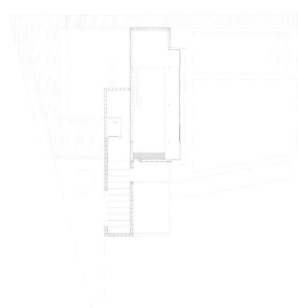

Opposite, top: A large circular cutout brings light down to the garage entrance.

Opposite, bottom: Cross section.

Above: The black slate floors and whitewashed walls give the interior a stark, graphic quality. Aluminum louvers shade the large glass doors.

Left: Upper floor plan.

t house

Toyo Ito & Associates, Architects
Tokyo, Japan 1999

Living and working under the same roof is becoming more and more commonplace. People choose to join the once completely distinct worlds of work and home for a variety of reasons. For some, it is mostly a matter of convenience: no arduous commute on crowded trains and buses, no getting stuck in traffic on the way to work. For parents, being close to their young children is not only convenient; the proximity may mean the difference between being able to work and not working at all. Combining workplace and home also has economic benefits if one can pool resources to make a single space for living and working instead of the split expenses of building and maintaining a home and office. Of course, there are potential pitfalls to such arrangements, primarily the lack of time and space boundaries between one's personal and professional obligations.

Japanese architect Toyo Ito faced these issues in creating a live-work space in Tokyo for a couple that owns a graphic design firm. Ito, known for lightweight, luminous buildings and structures, like his Tower of Winds (1986), a piece of urban sculpture in Yokohama, and his Sendai Mediatheque (2001) in northern Japan, designed a two-story structure with a similarly ethereal facade.

The couple makes few distinctions between time spent working, sleeping, eating, and relaxing; nor do they make strict divisions of space for one type of activity versus another. So Ito decided that flexibility was the proper solution, with domestic and work areas commingled. He organized the 148-square-meter (1,595-square-foot) house on two levels. One enters the house laterally, into a double-height entry hall separating the child's bedroom and the garage at the front of the house from the master bedroom and baths at the rear. Upstairs are the living room, studio, and

kitchen. A concrete staircase built into the side of the concrete-walled structure leads to a rooftop deck.

The structure and materials are kept simple and utilitarian. The long sides of the rectangular plan are defined by a series of seismically stable walls of poured concrete, divided by slots of double-height gridded windows. The street elevation is the most elegant and mysterious, and most reminiscent of the material sleight of hand that makes Ito's work seem ethereal. The architect clad the short facade in horizontal bands of translucent glass, except for a solid garage door on the ground level and a tiny square window with clear glass that seemingly interrupts the clean horizontal composition. The window, in fact, offers a glimpse of a cherry tree, a neighborhood landmark, just in front of the house, and frames a small sliver of the view outside like a piece of art hung on the wall. Inside, Ito stuck to basic materials: concrete and wood floors, wood cabinetry, and a folded industrial metal staircase.

The language of vertical windows and, especially, the translucent glass street facade brings to mind traditional Japanese shoji screens. But instead of a delicate teahouse, Ito toughened up the workaday home and office with no-nonsense materials. From the outside, it is a polite, discrete neighbor. On the inside, it handles the demands of a busy work and family life.

Previous spread: The entrance is through large doors surrounded by vertical windows on opposite sides of the house.

Above left: A square window with clear glass frames a view of a favorite cherry tree like a work of art.

Above right: The entry hall is a soaring double-height space that leads to a live-work space upstairs.

Opposite: The street elevation is a cool, neutral composition with bands of translucent glass interrupted by garage doors and a small square window on the second floor.

Opposite, top left: The entrance to the house is along one of two narrow walkways at the sides of the house.

Opposite, top right: Translucent panels slide to create privacy in the live/work space at the front of the house.

Opposite, bottom left: Side elevation (top); longitudinal section (middle); second-floor plan (bottom).

Opposite, bottom right: The translucent glass skin produces shadows that animate a spare, minimalist room.

Right: Conceptual axonometric.

Below: The second-floor stair landing separates a kitchen and dining space at the rear of the house (left) from the live/work space at right.

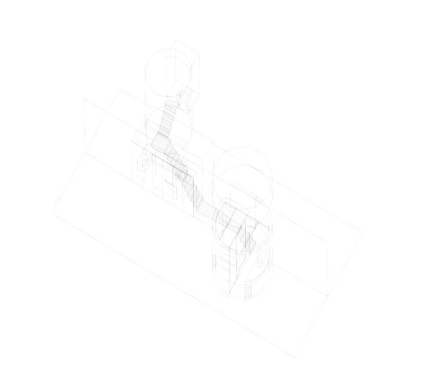

c house and y house

Kei'ichi Irie, Power Unit Studio
Tokyo and Chita-Shi, Japan 2001

Around the world, populations are aging while cities continue to expand. In Tokyo, space has always been at a premium. Young adults typically live with their parents until marriage, given the lack of available, affordable housing in and close to the city. Many households are finding themselves with children, parents, and grandparents—and even the complete families of grown siblings—living under the same roof.

That was the case with the owner of a food company and his wife who commissioned architect Kei'ichi Irie of Power Unit Studio to build a house in Tokyo's Arakawa district. The clients, who used to live with the families of the husband's two brothers, now share their 108-square-meter (1,163-square-foot) home with their three children and the husband's elderly mother. Irie had to fit comfortable living quarters for the three generations on a tight urban site. His design includes plenty of bedroom space and even a private courtyard. Irie says he wanted to maximize shared living space even if that meant smaller bedrooms for the family members, who were used to living in tight quarters.

The architect turned the house perpendicular to the road; a short, solid wall with a small projecting volume comprise the street elevation. To one side is the private access court, which allowed Irie to install

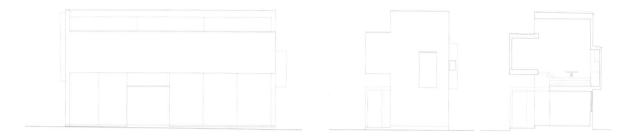

Previous spread: The C House
offers an unexpectedly
open facade in a crowded Tokyo
neighborhood.

Above: Entry facade elevation
(left), street elevation (center),
rear elevation (right).

Right: The narrow street facade
is completely opaque.
The master bedroom cantilevers
over the entry, at left.

Opposite: An open space
adjoining the house allows for
clear glass along the length of
the entry facade. A corrugated
metal canopy shelters the front
door.

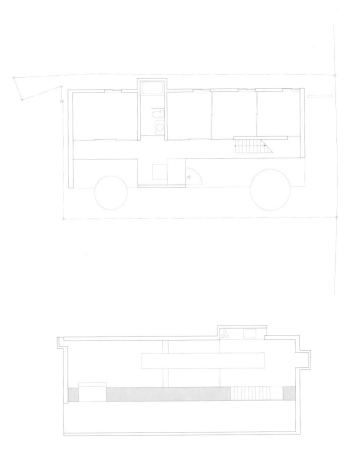

Opposite: The home's most innovative feature is a long glass table extending from the kitchen to the living area, with multiple functions along its length.

Above: Ground-floor plan (top); second-floor plan (bottom).

floor-to-ceiling panes of glass on the lower-level facade that let light into the narrow house without sacrificing privacy. The front door, also made of glass, is sheltered beneath an L-shaped canopy of corrugated metal that appears to extend inside the house through the glazed facade. The ground floor opens up to a double-height volume that allows views up to the second-floor living and dining area.

The lower level contains four bedrooms, three for the children and one for their grandmother, separated by a shared bath. Irie says the layout reminded him of sleeping compartments on a train. Each has a small window overlooking a narrow alley between the house and its neighbors. Upstairs is an open living space that extends the full length of the house. To keep the clean lines of the open living space uninterrupted, Irie recessed the small kitchen into the rear wall. Most of this linear whitewashed space is taken up by a long glass table, the focus of shared life for the three generations in the home. While the table height remains continuous, the floor level beneath it steps up subtly to allow different functions to take place along a single surface: kitchen counter at the far end, Western-style dining table in the middle, and, this being Japan, a low table with traditional floor seating at the far end. As the architect points out, the change in floor level changes the function of the glass table, but the divisions between those functions remain invisible.

At the far end of the space, along a bright orange wall that provides the only punch of color in an otherwise cool, neutral interior, two short steps of stainless-steel mesh bridge the double-height void to reach the master suite. The parents' bedroom takes up the entire length of the house. Unlike the glass entry wall beneath it, the long cantilevered volume is completely opaque, although a clerestory running its full length brings daylight into the upstairs living space. A small window at the back of the bedroom brings in its own source of light.

In a very small amount of space, Irie was able to create separate and distinct areas for all of the home's occupants. Even though the children's bedrooms are not far from the grandmother's, the shared bathroom between them gives her a small degree of separation from her charges. The parents enjoy their own separate realm, which is just steps from living areas but feels completely isolated. Irie's clever use of the long glass dining table as the dominant focal point of the shared living area recognizes the fact that meals are a rare opportunity for busy families to come together, and the dining table celebrates the event. His design is specific for a particular family and a particular site in crowded Tokyo, but it offers lessons for families of all sizes and compositions on maintaining personal space as well as sharing experiences while living under the same roof.

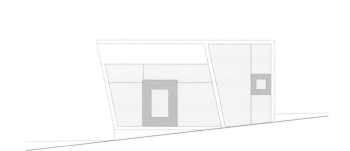

Previous spread: The rear facade reveals the shape that gives the Y House its name.

Opposite, top left: Entry facade elevation.

Opposite, top right: A long trapezoidal window in the top-floor bedroom overlooks the living/dining space below.

Opposite, bottom: The long window in the bedroom looks back at the entrance.

Above: A glass door with a thick black frame leads from the living/dining room to a terrace at the back of the house.

Right: Top-level plan (top); middle-level plan (bottom).

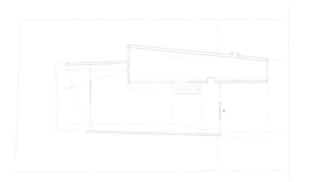

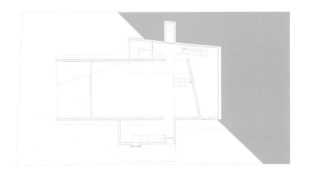

Irie designed another, more unorthodox house he calls the Y House in the town of Chita-Shi, near Nagoya. The clients are a product designer in a large corporation and the owner of a furniture import company. There are obvious differences between the two projects. "The C House is cubic space in a city; the Y House has freeform angles overlooking nature," says Irie. "The reason I made slanted walls is to avoid any reflection, influence, or restriction from solid walls facing each other."

From the back, the house indeed resembles a large Y that embraces a precious patch of open land. As one enters through a small, translucent glass-faced structure at the uppermost level, there's no indication of the striking structure to come. The three levels cover just 135 square meters (1,445 square feet). The top level contains the entry foyer and a bedroom; the lower level, the largest of the three, contains the

kitchen and an open living/dining room; and the bottom level houses a second bedroom.

The most dramatic interior is the long open space that cantilevers out into the site above the solid basement level. This large open living/dining room ends in a wall of glass that opens onto a small terrace overlooking a wooded area. A large canted window along one side brings in daylight as it pushes into the kinetic space, whose walls and even a corner of the floor bend up and out.

The reinforced concrete floors, walls, and roofs that allowed the architect to shape the home's distinctive profile all measure 150 mm thick. Irie says it was difficult to create such a thin concrete section because of the seismic reinforcement necessary in Japan. But he needed a structural and conceptual thinness and lightweight construction. "I wanted the house to be like a paper wrapper, not a solid box," says Irie.

Above: Built-in stairs lead from the top-floor entry foyer to the living/dining space one flight below. The kitchen is at the rear.

Opposite, top: The rear facade reveals the home's unusual geometry and daring concrete structure.

Opposite, bottom left: Exposed tie holes create a pattern in the concrete walls.

Opposite, bottom right: Longitudinal section.

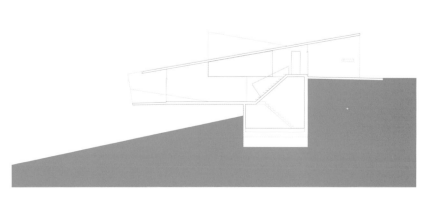

dirty house

David Adjaye, Adjaye/Associates
London, United Kingdom 2002

British artists Tim Noble and Sue Webster made a splash in 1996 with their first solo exhibition, titled "British Rubbish." Since then, the couple has gained notoriety with sculptures made of mounds of rubbish and wall-mounted reliefs with silhouettes in light bulbs and neon strips. Their work has a tough, urban, almost punk sensibility. The live-work house that architect David Adjaye of Adjaye/Associates designed for them in East London seems well suited to their work. It also fits in with the rough-and-tumble, dirty streets of this gentrifying but still ragged neighborhood—hence the home's name, Dirty House—where the city's lively contemporary art scene is flourishing in cutting-edge galleries and trendy bars and restaurants.

Adjaye, who has earned a loyal following among such young British contemporary artists as Chris Ofili for buildings that bridge the divide between art and architecture, started with an empty two-story warehouse. He painted the thick brick walls black on the outside and fitted reflective glass into two rows of large square windows in the masonry shell. On the ground floor, the glazing is flush with the outside surface of the punched opening; on the second floor, the

glass is recessed within the square opening, giving a contrasting sense of the wall's thickness. Inside the lowermost floors is a pair of soaring, 20-foot-high (6-meter-high) studio spaces, a study, and a guest suite.

Above the heavy brick base, Adjaye inserted a new one-story glass-enclosed structure containing a loft-like living space with a completely open kitchen, living, and dining area and a more private bedroom and bathroom suite separated from the open living space by a wall of closets. The glass penthouse is partially concealed from the street by the parapet extending up from the brick base and set back from the brick walls on two sides to create a shallow terrace. Seen from the street, the white roof, which extends beyond the glass skin, seems to float above the black box of the base, an effect made more dramatic at night when the underside of the roof is lit by the glow of the interior lights through the floor-to-ceiling glass facade. The total square footage of the house is 465 square meters (5,000 square feet).

Ajdaye's strategy works well with the reality of the scruffy neighborhood. At the street, the house is solid and seemingly impenetrable; inside, the couple works surrounded by towering whitewashed space focused inward, not outward. On the uppermost level where they live, the house takes on a lightweight, open character, filled with light from the floor-to-ceiling glass wall on two sides, as well as from a large skylight above the living space, which pays homage

Previous spread: The house was converted from a reclaimed brick factory building in East London, with a new penthouse level on top.

Above: A parapet wall protects the floor-to-ceiling glass skin of the new rooftop living areas.

Opposite, top: The house turns a solid, protective face to the neighborhood, but the illuminated underside of the roof atop the new penthouse level suggests a lighter, brighter space.

Opposite, bottom left: Despite its striking appearance, the house blends in with the scale and window patterns of its neighbors.

Opposite, bottom right: The roof of the top-floor addition floats above the two-story black masonry base.

Opposite: Behind the painted brick facade is a bright, white-washed double-height space.

Above left: The top-floor living spaces are crowned by a large skylight and surrounded by glass walls.

Above right: Strip fluorescent lights above the living-dining area suggest the minimalist art of Dan Flavin.

Right: Section (right); top-floor plan (left).

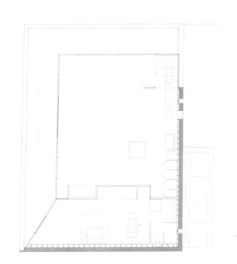

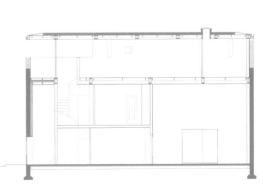

to the "sky spaces" of California artist James Turrell. Strips of simple fluorescent tubes placed end-to-end across the open space recall the 1970s neon installations of the minimalist artist Dan Flavin.

Indeed, with its abstractly detailed base and gossamer crown, the home itself looks like a minimalist, monolithic sculpture tucked among the shabby brick warehouses of the East End. Even though he opened up the living space to the light and the views of London's rooftops, Adjaye keeps its inhabitants feeling protected by the parapet and the sheltering roof cantilever above.

Adjaye's longtime associations with young artists of his generation and his own interest in contemporary art have helped him develop a style that resonates with artists, architects, and clients outside of creative fields. His latest design proposal, a new building for the Museum of Contemporary Art in Denver, Colorado, will take that sensibility to a larger scale. Smaller residential work like the Dirty House demonstrates his ability to create architecture that is artful but still sensitive to the city of which it is a vital part.

Above left: The work areas, with towering ceilings and natural light, recall the lofty interiors of art galleries.

Top right: A black side door opens into the whitewashed studio spaces.

Above right: A narrow side yard leads to the ground-floor studios.

Opposite: Adjaye highlighted the thickness of the masonry base by making lower-level windows flush with the exterior skin and higher windows flush with the interior surface.

wall house 2

John Hejduk
Groningen, The Netherlands 2001

The influential American architect and longtime dean of the Irwin S. Chanin School of Architecture at the Cooper Union in New York, John Hejduk originally designed the Wall House 2 in 1973. Hejduk created the design for a landscape architect and fellow faculty member for a wooded site in Ridgefield, Connecticut, but the project was never built because of cost concerns. Hejduk died in 2000, but the city council of Groningen, The Netherlands, was committed to completing his well-known project, a sculptural exercise in cubist abstraction and functional theory. A local development company funded construction of the house as a speculative project. The completed home, overlooking a lake in the Hoomse Meer neighborhood, was eventually purchased. The developer made a few alterations in size (the built house is 20 percent larger than Hejduk's original design, now covering 265 square meters, or 2,851 square feet) and detailing to meet local building codes; otherwise the project remains true to Hejduk's conception.

The architect's guiding conceit was to celebrate and challenge conventional notions of what distinguishes living areas from functional ones—a twist on Louis Kahn's concept of "servant and served" spaces.

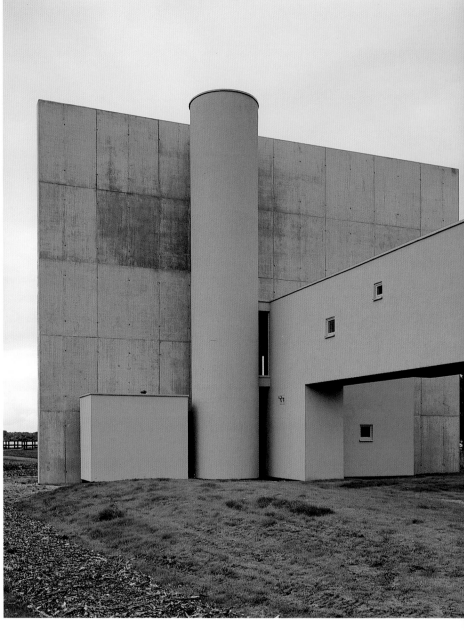

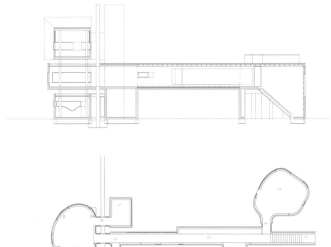

Previous spread: The Wall House is indeed organized around a wall, which separates living areas, to the right of the concrete slab, from more functional spaces. At far left is a studio.

Above left: Each level of the living wing follows its own fluid geometry, with differing arrangements of ribbon windows.

Above right: The colorful volumes contrast with the solid gray wall of concrete behind them.

Left: Longitudinal section (top); second-floor plan (middle). Cross section (bottom left); elevation (bottom right).

Opposite: The stacked living spaces, visually skewered with columns extending the full height of the house, contain separate functions: living room (top floor), kitchen and dining room (middle floor), and bedroom (bottom floor).

For Wall House 2, Hejduk defined the less pragmatic areas of the house as the bedroom, kitchen and dining room, and living room; the more straightforwardly functional zones include the bathrooms, stairs, and a studio. The living spaces are housed in fluid, irregularly shaped volumes wrapped in curving ribbon windows and stacked atop each other, with the kitchen and dining room on the middle level (the entry level), the living room on the top floor, and the bedroom on the ground. The living room is painted deep yellow, the kitchen/dining room pale pink, and the bedroom mint green. Hejduk visually severed these colorful, freeform living spaces from the home's functional areas—which are contained within a long, almost completely solid bridge—with a towering concrete wall that slices the living spaces like a giant guillotine.

The one glaring exception to Hejduk's forceful separation of program elements is the studio, located at the opposite end of the service bar from the tower-like stack of living spaces. The studio, painted a pale melon color, is even more freeform in plan, appearing almost biomorphic. It floats one level above the ground, supported on one round and one square column and accessible by its own staircase from the ground. One could question if the studio is any more pragmatic than the kitchen, which is ganged with the living and dining and bedroom areas. But its position keeps the entire composition anchored and off-balance, giving the house an extra jolt of visual and conceptual energy.

Hejduk wanted occupants to feel the difference between the spaces on either side of the wall. To wit,

the interiors could not be more radically distinct. The living spaces feel like cocoons bubbling outward with tensile energy. Both the walls and windows undulate, each with its own rhythmic energy. The top-floor living room follows a more classically Corbusian model, with a continuous ribbon of windows wrapping the entire piano curve of the structure. The windows of the ground-floor bedroom, by comparison, swell up and down, creating energetic freeform frames for views of the nearby lake. The window pattern on the intermediary kitchen and dining floor is somewhere between the glazing on the floors below and above it, with changes in the depth and length of the windows along the course of the perimeter.

As if the change in spatial quality were not enough to register the differences between the two extremes, Hejduk also marks the passage through the dividing wall clearly. Tall, narrow slot windows encountered just before one passes from the functional wing into the living areas call attention to the transition.

In nearly 35 years of practice, Hejduk did not build many projects; nonetheless, his career was highly influential to generations of students. The Wall House is a rare glimpse into Hejduk's theories writ large and in concrete. And now that the project has finally been built, one can experience the clarity and forcefulness of his ideas in the realm of the private house. They are provocative ideas, and the rooms inside the house sophisticated spaces.

Opposite: The studio is far removed from the tower of functional spaces, but given a similar exterior treatment. The studio is located at the end of the long solid bar extending from the guillotine-like wall dividing living and functional areas of the house.

Above left: A lyrical variation in window design compliments the undulating facade.

Above right: An enclosed staircase leads up to the solid bridge at the second level, which passes through the dividing wall to reach the kitchen and living room and other, more ceremonial spaces above and below.

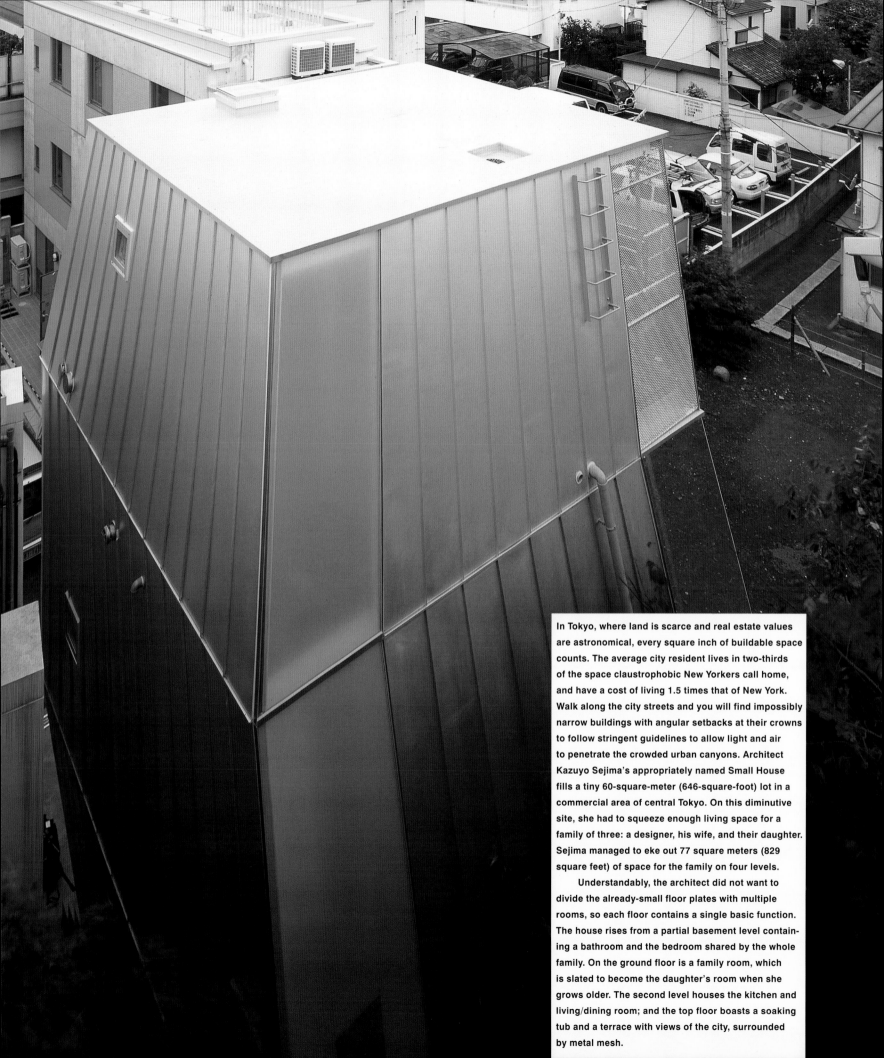

In Tokyo, where land is scarce and real estate values are astronomical, every square inch of buildable space counts. The average city resident lives in two-thirds of the space claustrophobic New Yorkers call home, and have a cost of living 1.5 times that of New York. Walk along the city streets and you will find impossibly narrow buildings with angular setbacks at their crowns to follow stringent guidelines to allow light and air to penetrate the crowded urban canyons. Architect Kazuyo Sejima's appropriately named Small House fills a tiny 60-square-meter (646-square-foot) lot in a commercial area of central Tokyo. On this diminutive site, she had to squeeze enough living space for a family of three: a designer, his wife, and their daughter. Sejima managed to eke out 77 square meters (829 square feet) of space for the family on four levels.

Understandably, the architect did not want to divide the already-small floor plates with multiple rooms, so each floor contains a single basic function. The house rises from a partial basement level containing a bathroom and the bedroom shared by the whole family. On the ground floor is a family room, which is slated to become the daughter's room when she grows older. The second level houses the kitchen and living/dining room; and the top floor boasts a soaking tub and a terrace with views of the city, surrounded by metal mesh.

Sejima's inventiveness comes through in the home's kinetic glass and galvanized metal enclosure. The only regular geometric element is the steel-framed stair tower slicing through the center of the house with the spiral stair connecting the disparate floors. The sculptural profile of the exterior recedes and flows out according to how much space the architect wanted to allocate to each function and each floor within the site's buildable footprint. The semi-submerged bedroom level is the smallest; the entry floor above flares out from the basement-level footprint, the painted steel struts supporting the concrete floor slab angling outward to accommodate the slab of the larger living floor above. At the top-floor roof deck level, the skin angles in again to crown the compact house. By pinching in the footprint of the basement-level bedrooms, she was able to squeeze in a ground-floor parking space near the front door.

Sejima clad the west elevation in continuous sheets of glass and part of the south-facing entry facade in frosty translucent glass—except the terrace level, which is wrapped in industrial mesh fencing. The glass lets the owners look out onto a small patch of unbuilt land adjoining their property, a breath of fresh air in congested Tokyo. She skinned the rest of the exterior in galvanized metal, in part to conceal the services such as plumbing chases on the east side of the house.

Fitting in the bare minimum of space needed for an urban family to live comfortably on this site was challenging enough. Sejima was able to deftly accomplish that with a sublime, energetic design. And she was able to plan for the not-too-distant future, when the young daughter will want and need her own sleeping space. Even in the crowded confines of Tokyo, some functions are elemental.

Opposite, top: Canted walls of floor-to-ceiling glass create a dynamic interior space.

Opposite, bottom: The spiral stair at its center, surrounded by a thick steel structure, is the only continuous element in the house.

Above: Though compact, the living spaces receive plenty of daylight and even an unobstructed view of the sky.

Previous spread, left page: Different-sized floor plates wrapped in glass give the Small House its unusual profile. Right page: The back facades of the house are solid, to screen out adjoining houses in the dense Tokyo neighborhood and to conceal plumbing chases and other mechanical equipment.

private house

Will Bruder Architects
Pride's Crossing, Massachusetts, United States 2000

Phoenix architect Will Bruder is the consummate desert modernist. Bruder, who studied sculpture in his native Wisconsin, trained with the visionary architect and utopian planner Paolo Soleri in the Arizona desert and later opened a studio in the mountains outside Phoenix in 1974. His Phoenix Central Library, which opened in 1995, embodies his ideas about creating modern, even high-tech architecture rooted in the elemental desert landscape. For instance, towering copper-clad "saddlebag" service cores recall the copper-colored sides of desert rock formations. Bruder has designed scores of houses throughout the American Southwest that engage their arid landscapes with combinations of hard-edged and organic forms, as well as libraries and museums in Scottsdale, Arizona; Jackson, Wyoming; and Reno, Nevada.

The setting for Bruder's first project outside the West is a far cry from the desert hills of Arizona: a rocky 3-hectare (8-acre) site on the coast of Massachusetts overlooking the Atlantic Ocean. The architect designed a large compound for a large family, with the new main house, a renovated carriage house, an exercise pavilion, and several follies located throughout the large property. Bruder began the process by demolishing an existing Italianate villa from the early twentieth century and developing a master plan that met the client's needs while responding to the topography and views of the site.

Previous spread: The home's low profile and long stone walls make it blend into its rocky costal setting.

Opposite, left: A long hallway flanked by glass walls leads from the entrance to the living spaces.

Opposite, top right: A curving wall wraps a fireplace with textured panels of cast white bronze, a piece by artist Darcy Miro.

Opposite, bottom right: The kitchen counters follow the home's curving geometries.

Above: Along the entire rear facade, large panes of glass open the house up to the surrounding gardens.

The plan of the 604-square-meter (6,500-square-foot) main house recalls the fluid floor plans of Bruder's early work, which in turn owes something to the organicism of Soleri and the American architect Bruce Goff. An entry drive leads to a circular driveway with an old beech tree at its center; the house unfolds as a series of overlapping crescents following the curve of the entry drive, as well as the curve of the hillside as it slopes down toward the ocean. A vaulted entry hallway slices through the crescents, connecting the disparate wings of the house.

The outermost layer contains a three-car garage to the left of the entry foyer, a sleek glass pavilion crowned by an angular stainless steel canopy. The middle layer contains two distinct zones on opposite sides of the entry hall: a long, arcing hallway with a study, three children's bedrooms with private bathrooms, a recreation room that opens onto a terrace at the far end; and a service area with a laundry room and a guest suite beyond. Tucked between the bedroom wing and the living pavilion at the rear of the house is a black-bottomed reflecting pool made of stainless steel. Opposite the living area, an open space with an arcing open kitchen at its center, is the sprawling master suite with a spacious bath and dressing area and a corner wall of glass that offers views of the water from the bed. Beyond the outermost layer is a large terraced garden sloping down to the sea.

Bruder's unorthodox plan has the atmosphere of a small village. Its sophisticated layering of space creates almost urban outdoor spaces, such as the reflecting pool between the bedroom and living wings, which has the feeling of a vest-pocket park squeezed into a tiny space on a city street. By organizing distinct functions in concentric rings of space, he maximized privacy for the family. The long bedroom wing, with its own shared activity space, keeps the children removed from the parent's bedroom.

The palette is a mix of sleek, polished materials and rustic elements bound beneath the gentle arcs of the roof planes, which echo the geometry of the segmented floor plans. The solid walls of the exterior are clad in hefty blocks of granite that tie the house to the rocky landscape, and contrast with stretches of floor-to-ceiling glass sheltered by shiny steel canopies. The juxtaposition of massive walls of stone with planes of glass joined with thin metal mullions creates a dynamic dialog between solid and void, open and closed. The walls give the house a sense of shelter and enclosure—as does Bruder's freeform organic plan—that makes the large windows feel like serendipitous modern insertions into an old stone barn, or a cave. It's a deft combination of rustic and sleek that shows that Bruder, the ultimate desert architect, can adapt the lessons of building modern houses in the arid West to the New England coast.

Top: Floor plan.

Above: Site plan.

Opposite, top: Mostly solid walls of granite wrap around a circular entry drive along the front of the house.

Opposite, bottom: An angular stainless-steel canopy crowns the glass-enclosed entry.

Top left: A curved desk in a small study off the master bedroom overlooks the ocean.

Top right: An elliptical dining table follows the curved floor plan, with tall windows overlooking the view.

Above right: A view down a corridor off the bedroom reveals the winding geometry of Bruder's plan.

Opposite: The living room at the back of the house opens onto views of the landscape through floor-to-ceiling walls of glass.

In 1999, New York architect Toshiko Mori, now chair of
the architecture department of the Harvard Graduate
School of Design, designed a guest annex to a 1957
house by Paul Rudolph on Casey Key near Sarasota,
Florida. The narrow barrier island, located between the
Gulf of Mexico to the west and Little Sarasota Bay to
the east, has only 400 houses—most of the 8-mile-long
key is a nature preserve. Three years later, Mori completed another project on Casey Key, with a main
house, guest house, and pool structure on a long,
narrow property stretching east to west between the
gulf and the bay. Mori's latest project respects the
island's delicate ecology as well as the unlikely but
important modernist legacy of the area.

In the late 1940s and early 1950s, the architects
Paul Rudolph and Ralph Twitchell designed a series of
influential buildings in the Sarasota area. In these
buildings, Rudolph and Twitchell created a strong
modern style based on the local vernacular, which was
geared toward keeping houses shaded and naturally
ventilated. Their work defined what came to be known
as the Sarasota School. Projects like the Walker Guest
House on Sanibel Island and the seminal Cocoon
House on Siesta Key lift above the ground on platforms to help cool the house and protect it from flood-
ing so close to the shore. In later projects, Rudolph
and Twitchell moved away from a delicate language of
wooden louvers to more monumental houses with towering walls of concrete block.

Mori's work on Casey Key followed something
of a similar path. Her first project, the guest house
adjoining the original Rudolph house, floats above the
tropical landscape on slender concrete columns; walls
of louvers recall the facades of Rudolph's Cocoon
House. Mori's most recent project is more monolithic,
though still respectful of the needs of building in
coastal Florida, especially raising the house above the
sand and shading windows and walls of glass from
the strong sun while opening up to the ocean views.
Like Rudolph's later work, the house plays solid walls
of concrete block against broad expanses of glass as
well as narrow slot windows.

Previous spread: The concrete-block structure of the main house commands an imposing view from the entry drive.

Above: A huge skylight crowns the staircase leading to the vast open living spaces on the second level.

Right: The glass-enclosed staircase connecting the ground floor with the living areas one flight up presents a dramatic view. A glass floor surrounding the stair brings light down to the ground floor.

Opposite, top: Middle-level plan (left); section (right).

Opposite, bottom: Narrow windows in the concrete-block walls provide slivers of sunlight and glimpses of the tropical vegetation.

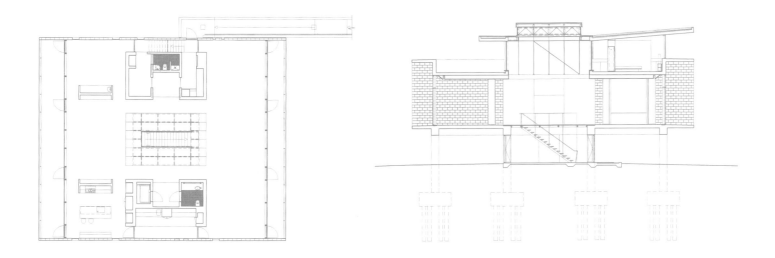

Located at the center of the site, the 623-square-meter (6,700-square-foot) main house is a large, stout, square structure raised above the sandy ground on concrete pilings. The concrete stilts keep the house above damaging flood waters and storm surges. The long-span concrete beams supporting the structure look worthy of a freeway overpass—such a hefty structural frame clearly helps withstand hurricane winds. One enters through a glass-enclosed vestibule beneath the house and moves inside the house along a minimalist staircase or up a small elevator. (There is also a long ramp that leads directly from the main floor toward the bay.)

The interior is a double-height open space with functional cores containing the stairs and elevator, bathrooms, storage, and laundry facilities at the center of the plan and facades of floor-to-ceiling glass doors and walls along the east and west sides. Small balconies extend the length of the house. These glass facades brighten the interior; deep overhangs control excess sunlight. To one side of the core is a soaring open kitchen and dining area; to the other side is a

living room. Upstairs are two bedrooms, sheltered beneath a gently sloping butterfly roof, with access to a roof deck.

Mori repurposed an old dormitory that existed on the gulf side of the property, once the site of a Coast Guard station, and turned it into a two-bedroom, 125-square-meter (1,350-square-foot) guest house among the sea grass and dunes. She added the pool house and pool along the edge of the bay, sheltered by a grove of citrus trees.

The site planning ensures privacy for the owners as well as their guests, with individual precincts for each outlined by the dense tropical landscape. Her interior planning makes the house a kind of tropical loft, an open, unprogrammed space that lends itself to the relaxed lifestyle its owners want for beachside living. All of the necessities are considered and carefully concealed within the service cores so the rest of the house can be kept as open and uncluttered as possible. Like Rudolph and Twitchell's pioneering houses of fifty years ago, Mori combines common sense with sensitivity to the coastal landscape and climate.

Above: Despite its large size, walls of glass and pilotis that raise it up off the sand make the house feel less intrusive in its tropical beachside setting.

Opposite, top: Tall glass doors along the open living/dining space access a terrace shaded by the roof overhang.

Opposite, bottom: Floor-to-ceiling glass surrounds the ground-floor lobby, creating a transparent vestibule next to the beach.

Above: An illuminated concrete ramp connects the main level of the house to the beach, keeping the entry stair free of sand.

Opposite, top left: Glass surrounding the entry stair creates a light feeling.

Opposite, bottom left: Beyond the entry stair, a dining table on axis opens up to views through a wall of windows.

Opposite, bottom right: A hefty concrete structure, designed to withstand hurricanes, lifts the house above the flood-prone ground plane.

suitcase house

Gary Chang, EDGE Design Institute
Badaling, Great Wall, China 2002

Architect Gary Chang of the Hong Kong firm Edge Design designed one of the eleven houses and clubhouse comprising the Commune by the Great Wall, a community of villas by a younger generation of Asian architects in Badaling, China, a 40-minute drive from Beijing. (See also Bamboo Wall House by Kengo Kuma, page 166.) The community, built by the Beijing development company SOHO China, Ltd. and located near the famous Great Wall, is being built in two stages. The houses built during the first phase operate as an environmentally friendly 100-room boutique hotel; the next stage will feature private weekend homes.

From the outside, the 347-square-meter (3,734-square-foot) house appears to be a staid timber-clad box with rows of vertical windows resting atop a solid base. Inside, however, it reveals itself as a dynamic, highly adaptable reimagining of private rooms in a traditional house. As its name suggests, the house contains a series of compartments—in this case, compartments fit for human occupation. Instead of proper rooms, Chang designed several dozen subterranean sleeping zones along the perimeter of the house, which are accessed by pneumatically hinged wood panels concealed as part of the floor. The

below-deck quarters recall the compartments of a small ship. Chang describes the concept as questioning the traditional image of the house and an attempt to rethink the nature of intimacy, privacy, spontaneity, and flexibility. He calls his design "a simple demonstration of the desire for ultimate adaptability in pursuit of a proscenium for infinite scenarios."

The interior transforms itself completely depending on the number of inhabitants and how much privacy they seek. The space can be kept open to create a lofty 5-meter-by-44-meter room, or divided into smaller spaces with folding wood partitions that glide along tracks in the ceiling. The floor hatches can be opened as desired to reveal sleeping quarters—up to seven guest rooms accommodating 14 people—as well as bathrooms, a kitchen, storage, and spaces for more specialized functions: a meditation chamber with a glass floor looking down the valley below, a music chamber, a library, a study, and a lounge. All of the chambers are located along the perimeter of the

long rectangular volume to make sure the occupants are never far from a window. The concrete base supporting the cantilevered main volume contains a pantry, maids' quarters, sauna, and mechanical room. Above the main living space is a roof terrace accessible by a pull-down staircase.

The exterior skin is wrapped in full height double-glazed folding doors that offer views of the Great Wall from every area of the interior (above ground, that is). To blur the distinctions between architecture, interior surfaces, and furniture, Chang clad the entire inside and outside of the steel and concrete structure in horizontal bands of timber siding.

There are few furnishings, mostly in the under-floor spaces. The spare furniture at floor level can be moved around, depending on the number and location of guests, for maximum flexibility. As the architect suggests, only the essential elements will be visible; everything else will be kept below deck, as it were, out of sight and out of mind.

Above: The architect wrapped the underside of the main volume in the same timber paneling used on the facades.

Opposite, top: The short end of the long rectangular house seems to float among the trees on the hillside site.

Opposite, bottom: A continuous band of tall windows along the facades opens up the interior to views of the surrounding landscape.

Previous spread: The wood-clad house cantilevers beyond its concrete base, visually floating above the rural landscape.

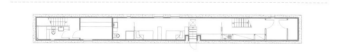

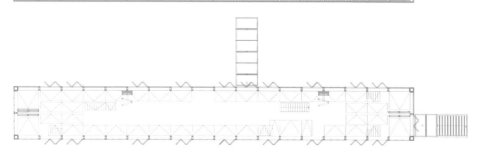

Above: Pneumatic hinges prop open the large trap doors that lead to sleeping quarters beneath the floor.

Left: Main-level plan (bottom); middle-level plan (center); bottom-level plan (top).

Opposite top: On the main level, furnishings are kept minimal and can be moved to accommodate flexible configurations of space.

Opposite bottom: The underfloor living and sleeping spaces are located near the perimeter windows to provide adequate natural light.

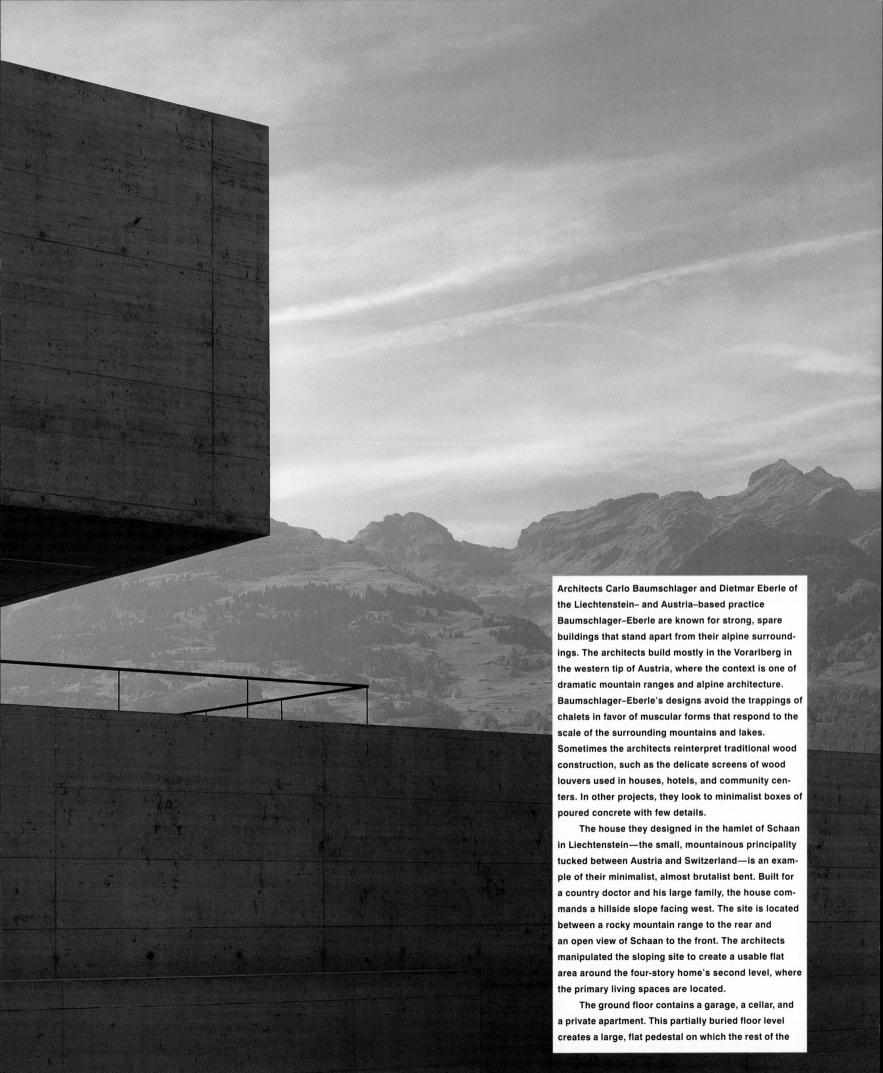

Architects Carlo Baumschlager and Dietmar Eberle of the Liechtenstein- and Austria-based practice Baumschlager-Eberle are known for strong, spare buildings that stand apart from their alpine surroundings. The architects build mostly in the Vorarlberg in the western tip of Austria, where the context is one of dramatic mountain ranges and alpine architecture. Baumschlager-Eberle's designs avoid the trappings of chalets in favor of muscular forms that respond to the scale of the surrounding mountains and lakes. Sometimes the architects reinterpret traditional wood construction, such as the delicate screens of wood louvers used in houses, hotels, and community centers. In other projects, they look to minimalist boxes of poured concrete with few details.

The house they designed in the hamlet of Schaan in Liechtenstein—the small, mountainous principality tucked between Austria and Switzerland—is an example of their minimalist, almost brutalist bent. Built for a country doctor and his large family, the house commands a hillside slope facing west. The site is located between a rocky mountain range to the rear and an open view of Schaan to the front. The architects manipulated the sloping site to create a usable flat area around the four-story home's second level, where the primary living spaces are located.

The ground floor contains a garage, a cellar, and a private apartment. This partially buried floor level creates a large, flat pedestal on which the rest of the

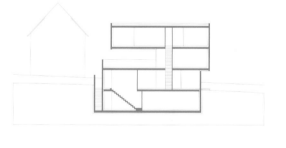

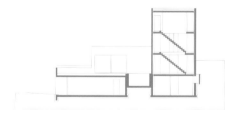

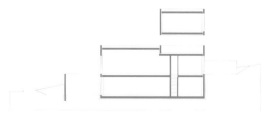

Previous spread: The pale yellow tint of the concrete echoes the muted tones of Liechtenstein's mountain ranges.

Opposite: The cantilevered top floor hangs over a lower volume to create a shady private terrace off the master bedroom.

Above left: The rear of the house opens onto a flattened lawn through sliding glass doors.

Above right: A concrete garden wall encloses a private pool.

Right: Longitudinal section (top); cross sections (center and bottom).

Opposite, top: Seen from the staircase, a wall of glass overlooks the open dining room and kitchen.

Opposite, bottom left: Sheer glass walls create a transparent stair hall connecting the home's three uppermost levels.

Opposite, bottom right: The architects carefully detailed the joints between stairs and glass.

Above: Large sliding glass doors open up the living spaces to views of the surrounding town of Schaan.

house sits comfortably. The entrance to the L-shaped main level, which houses shared living spaces, is along a flight of exterior stairs to the right of the garage. Sliding glass doors on two sides open onto small terraces and the flattened section of the hillside. Above the main living floor is the parents' floor, which maintains its privacy by turning a solid face to the street (and, unfortunately, to the view of the town), opening instead to the mountain view with large glass windows on the north and east sides. The west facade has a wall of sliding glass doors that lead to a private terrace, shaded by the long overhang of the children's wing above. The children's floor, meanwhile, has fewer windows, which face south toward Schaan and north toward the rocky mountain range behind the house. The total square footage for the house is 277 square meters (2,981 square feet).

Baumschlager–Eberle used pale concrete with a golden tint to construct the stacked, overlapping boxes that comprise the starkly minimalist house. They kept the detailing on the concrete exterior, including joints between panels and the patterning of tie-rod holes, simple. Rather than celebrate the construction process, they minimized its evidence so that what comes through most clearly is the simple organization of volumes, not surfaces. Inside, the detailing is also

spare: white plaster, pale wood, and green stone. The colors recall the palette of the surrounding mountainsides, with pine trees climbing up their rocky faces.

Though such a bold, bare house might seem jarring surrounded by more conservative chalets and villas, Baumschlager–Eberle's design is actually respectful of its context. Its scale is sympathetic to its neighbors; the fact that an entire floor level is buried into the hillside diminishes its bulk. And although the volumes pivot around the fixed base, the outdoor spaces created between blocks of concrete—the parents' private terrace, the entry court above the garage—are discrete. More importantly for this large family, the house is still roomy enough inside to create separate realms for parents and children and inviting spaces for them to share.

Above: The exposed profile of the staircase behind a glass wall becomes a sculptural object for the kitchen and dining area.

Right: Second floor plan.

Opposite: The home's main elevation reveals how comfortably the spare concrete volumes blend in with the houses and mountain landscape surrounding it.

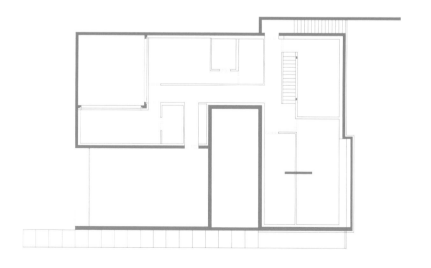

03 materials, craft and technology

Decades ago, if one were asked to imagine the homes in which we would live in the twenty-first century, high-tech structures worthy of NASA would surely come to mind—if not in outer space, then definitely earthbound homes built with space-age materials. Now that the twenty-first century has arrived, we know such futuristic houses are the exception, not the rule, if not simply the stuff of science fiction. The homes most people occupy are old-fashioned structures made of the same materials that have been used for centuries. The technology inside our homes, from televisions and audio systems to personal computers, evolves so quickly it's hard to keep pace. But the houses themselves stay hopelessly mired in the past.

Architects have certainly not abandoned the search for new materials, or at least innovative ways to build with time-honored materials. The Japanese architect Kengo Kuma used ancient bamboo to build a calming country house near the Great Wall in China (page 166). Understanding and even celebrating bamboo's brittle, fragile nature, Kuma created walls, floors, ceilings, and screens from the golden reeds. He played up bamboo's delicate, veil-like properties, creating diaphanous screens to enclose calm, contemplative spaces.

Another house in China, designed by architect Ma Qing Yun of MADA s.p.a.m for his father (page 170), uses one of the most basic of building materials, polished stones from local riverbeds, to create architecture very much of its place—literally. Local workers spent two years sifting for stones of varying sizes that the architect then used to cover the house and towering walls that enclose a large courtyard and smaller outdoor rooms. Two featured houses in Mexico also incorporate local materials into decidedly modern structures to create a link between architecture and its broader context. The F2 house by Adrià + Broid + Rojkind (page 172) is a striking concrete structure with dramatic open interiors and carefully framed views of the outdoors. To create a house that had resonance with the rich materials of Mexico, the architects lined walls in native volcanic basalt stone and finished floors in dark teak wood. The effect is a sophisticated combination of high-modern and rustic materials. The reconstruction of another house near Mexico City, the Pedernal House (page 198), by architect Adriana Monroy Noriega uses a similar mix of native materials to give a modern house local flavor. The original house, designed in the 1950s by Mexican architect Francisco Artigas, infused a local character into International Style modernism. Monroy Noriega continued Artigas's sensibility with dramatic walls of rough and textured stone.

London architects Sarah Wigglesworth and Jeremy Till used low-tech materials to create a unique and idiosyncratic but high-performance house. Wigglesworth and Till's own North London home and studio (page 192) features an ingenious combination of materials and construction techniques to minimize energy consumption and noise. Among the architects' more low-tech but efficient ideas are gabions filled with recycled chunks of concrete supporting the office wing, which absorbs vibrations from passing trains, and a wall of concrete-filled sandbags to minimize noise. Walls of bound straw bales covered in a corrugated skin of clear plastic and solid metal provide thick, inexpensive insulation on the north side of the home. Solar panels on the roof provide power, while large cisterns collect rainwater for re-use throughout the home.

German architect and engineer Werner Sobek looked to more high-performance systems in designing his own glass house in Stuttgart (page 186). The transparent four-story box looks deceptively simple. But everything about the home is carefully considered and exactly assembled, from the thermally efficient triple layer of glass with a plastic foil layer to reflect solar radiation but allow clear views, to the modular steel structure that was snapped together on site in just eleven days—and could be dismantled and re-used with a similarly quick turnaround. The home's sophisticated components include a heating and cooling system that takes advantage of the bright sunlight that fills the all-glass house. On a less technical but equally beneficial level, the house has no doorknobs or faucets; everything is controlled by computerized touch-pad or even voice-activated controls. Imagine the ease of walking through the front door by simply asking the door to open.

Like many architects' own homes, including Wigglesworth and Till's London residence and studio, Sobek's home is a kind of live-in laboratory, in this case for innovative structural, mechanical, and comfort systems. Living in such an experimental high-tech house may not be to everyone's liking, but it has singular elements that could be picked up on—touchless shower heads and kitchen cabinets, for instance.

Invisible technology and completely neutral materials can let architectural form shape the dominant image of a house. Such is the case with the Neugebauer House in Naples, Florida, by Richard Meier (page 204). Meier, who is more accustomed to building in cold climates, made the sunscreens that keep the home's waterfront glass facades an integral part of the architecture. The delicate scrims of louvers keep excess sun and heat from building up in the predominantly glass house, but don't distract from the clean lines of Meier's architecture, especially the striking butterfly roof that crowns the steel-framed structure.

The houses in this chapter represent some of the most innovative homes in terms of building materials, construction techniques, and residential technology. The particular solutions used by the architects depend on many factors: clients, program, site, and budget. But every one of them has interesting ideas that go well beyond their specific context.

Opposite: In a house in China by architect Ma Qing Yun of MADA s.p.a.m., smooth river stones set into concrete frames contrast with shutters covered in bamboo sheets.

Top: The Bamboo Wall House by Kengo Kuma utilizes reinforced bamboo rods to create delicate light-filtering screens.

Above: German architect Werner Sobek's house is an experimental high-tech glass box.

bamboo wall house

Kengo Kuma & Associates
Badaling, Great Wall, China 2002

This house designed by Japanese architect Kengo Kuma is part of the Commune by the Great Wall in Badaling, China, a 40-minute drive from Beijing. (See also Suitcase House by Gary Chang, page 150.) The planned community, the brainchild of the Beijing development company SOHO China, Ltd., includes eleven villas and a clubhouse designed by emerging Asian architects. The houses built in the first phase of the two-phase development function as a 100-room boutique hotel with an emphasis on environmental sustainability. Future houses will be used as private weekend homes.

Kuma took inspiration from the nearby Great Wall, whose formal qualities he admired. (The project's name, the Bamboo Wall House, reinforces its conception as a wall moving through the landscape as well as a house.) The Great Wall undulates wildly as it runs along an up-and-down ridgeline, seemingly forever; but it never registers as an object that is isolated from the landscape. Its wavelike profile follows the dips and peaks of the rolling terrain. Similarly, Kuma did not want to flatten the existing topography of the site he was given to build an object-like house. Instead, he designed the house as a long bar that extends to a lower level as the hillside slopes downward. The

Previous spread: The exterior contrasts polished glass with rough bamboo.

Top: The massing of the house follows the natural contours of the site, like the Great Wall on which the project is based.

Above left: Reflecting pools, bamboo overhangs, and walls that screen views of the landscape create a mystical atmosphere.

Above right: A glass-enclosed atrium leads to a meditative lounge surrounded by a shallow reflecting pool.

Opposite: The dining area features contrasting materials and textures: slate floors, glass walls, and bamboo walls, ceilings, and columns.

wall-like organization enhances the landscape, as Kuma suggests, instead of interfering with it.

Kuma wanted to use local materials as much as possible. Instead of the stone of the Great Wall, he decided on bamboo, an easily grown material that resonates culturally with both the Chinese and Japanese. He also found the material "charming" because of its brittleness and fragility. While the Great Wall itself is an impenetrable, solidly built barrier, the bamboo enclosure of Kuma's house is diaphanous and delicate. He used the material on many different surfaces: floors, walls, ceilings, and sunshades, as freestanding planes or as cladding over the steel-and-concrete structural system. The brittle material could not structurally support any loads, so in order to use the reeds as columns, Kuma inserted a steel angle reinforced with concrete inside the hollow stalk. Other materials harmonize with the golden bamboo: floors of local slate in the main living areas, tatami mats in the bedrooms, and plasterboard walls lined with Japanese paper.

The entry to the 716-square-meter (7,683-square-foot) house is at the upper level, up two sets of stairs and onto a long slate-floored porch shaded by a bamboo screen. The uppermost floor is shaped like an elongated U with an atrium at its center, rather like a Roman *impluvium* or courtyard, which functions as a contemplative lounge. To one side of the atrium are the living room, dining room, kitchen, and storage; to the other side are four bedrooms, two with private bathrooms and two with a shared bathroom off the hallway. Two additional bedrooms and staff and mechanical rooms are located on the lower level.

Kuma capitalized on bamboo's inherent properties to play up the effects of light and shadow, transparency and solidity, openness and privacy. These qualities are most evident in the atrium lounge, a self-contained outdoor space that has the calm, monastic feeling of a religious temple. Kuma placed the square lounge in a shallow reflecting pool like a floating platform anchored to the house by two narrow walkways. The walls and ceiling of unevenly spaced bamboo rods create irregular patterns of light and dark, acting as three-dimensional curtains framing selected views of the surrounding hillsides and subtly veiling others. Kuma's simple but sophisticated use of an ancient building element is a material as well as a poetic exploration.

Opposite: A slate-floored entry
porch flanked by a wall of
bamboo leads to the front door.

Above: Screens of irregularly
spaced bamboo rods surround
a contemplative open-air
lounge overlooking the mountain
landscape.

Right: Ground-floor plan.

f2 house

Adrià+Broid+Rojkind
Mexico City, Mexico 2001

This house by architects Miquel Adrià, Isaac Broid, and Michel Rojkind on the outskirts of Mexico City puts a warm, tactile spin on Modernism with rich local materials. The architects gave the three-level, 465-square-meter (5,000-square-foot) house a structural frame of steel and poured-in-place concrete which allowed them to create daring cantilevered spaces that defy structural logic. For instance, on the garden facade the concrete box of the second-level living room floats out beyond walls of glass. The exposed board-formed concrete wall bridges the material gap between the typical elements of Modernism—concrete, steel, and glass—and richer, more sculptural materials such as volcanic basalt stone, teak, and travertine.

The architects defined a private precinct for the house with long, towering walls of local basalt stone. One enters the L-shaped house on the middle of three levels, along a wooden path and through a doorway framed by dark stone walls and sheltered by a thin

Opposite: Long horizontal windows in the living room frame unexpected views of a shallow reflecting pool.

Above left: The entry facade, with stone walls sheltered by a thin roof canopy, belies the home's three-story structure.

Above right: A covered deck extends the length of the entry hall on the main level.

Right: Cross sections (top and bottom); longitudinal section (center).

Previous spread: By day and at night, the garden facade appears to be a structurally daring composition, with the concrete block of the living spaces visually suspended within walls of glass above and below.

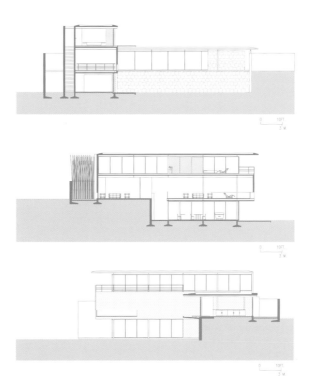

travertine canopy on slender columns. The dark masonry walls flanking the front door conceal a service zone at the front of the house. Just inside the home is an open kitchen and dining room, overlooking a glass wall with a long, shaded terrace overlooking a garden one level below; beyond is a cozy den and, in the shorter leg of the L-shaped plan, a large living room. Directly below the living room is a shared family room with sliding glass doors on two sides that open onto a small terrace and a broad lawn. Above the living room is the bedroom level, with the master suite and two smaller bedrooms with a shared bath. All of the bedrooms open onto a deck wrapping two sides of the house.

The exteriors of the house are primarily exposed concrete, with its mottled board-formed texture, painted steel columns, floor-to-ceiling glass, and black basalt rock wrapping the home's perimeter and retaining walls. Inside, the palette is much the same, as the architects left the structure exposed. There are also rich polished floors of teak and crosscut travertine and walls covered in wenge wood.

The unexpected adjacencies and residual spaces created by the home's complex intertwining of volumes are among its best assets. Adrià, Broid, and Rojkind inserted a shallow reflecting pool with a rough stone bottom between the main-floor den and the stone wall defining the edge of the site behind the house. As in other spaces in the house, the view from the den toward the reflecting pool is unconventional, framed

for dramatic effect: A single long, narrow window is set low against the floor, creating an abstract, focused view of the reflecting pool. Another narrow window is placed perpendicular to the floor, offering a vertical slice of the basalt-stone garden wall. The architects used a similar technique at the garden end of the living room, where a large square window projects out from the concrete wall to frame a view of the landscape like a work of art on the wall. Another low window hugs the floor and wraps the corner, revealing a column outside. The visual weight seems upended; the concrete wall appears to sit atop a glass base, defying gravity and the laws of physics.

A similar structural play exists on the exterior. The living room volume, wrapped in walls of textured concrete, projects out beyond the glass skin wrapping the entire facade around it. Because the supporting columns are placed inside the glass skin, the optical effect is that the concrete box is floating above and beneath glass voids.

The great unifying space is the slender skylit stair hall that extends along the side wall of the house, from the den to the living room. The hall is a narrow sunlit chasm capped by a skylight. The rooms that flank it are open to the void, including the master bedroom, where a notch cut into the concrete side wall lets sunlight and space bleed between the bedroom and stair hall.

The F2 House, so titled for the surname of the couple that owns it, is an amazingly sophisticated house. It is strikingly modern, but its thoughtful use of warm natural materials, especially the volcanic stone typical of Mexico, keeps it tied to the culture of its site.

Above: A dynamic arrangement of windows in the concrete wall of the living room frames views of the surrounding landscape.

Opposite: A notched concrete wall in the master bedroom overlooks the skylit stair hall.

father's house on jade mountain

MADA s.p.a.m.
Xi'an, China 2003

The towering mountain peaks of north-central China's Shaanxi Province, the natural topographical barrier dividing northern and southern China, have figured prominently in the country's moody, mystical landscape painting for at least 1,000 years. The early artist and Shaanxi native Fan Kuan captured the region's misty elevations in his famous work *Travelling Amid Mountains and Gorges*, dating from about 1000 A.D. Painters were drawn to what still exists in the area: one of the world's most biologically diverse forest lands, with hillsides covered in native firs, ginkgos, yews, and bamboo that supports the indigenous population of the world-famous Giant Pandas.

At the foot of Qinlin Mountain near the ancient Chinese capital of Xi'an—the starting point of the legendary Silk Road and home to the famous terra cotta soldiers of the Qin Dynasty—architect Ma Qing Yun of MADA s.p.a.m designed a house for his father that responds to the area's natural allure. (The name of the Shanghai-based practice, founded by Yun in 1999, is an acronym for Strategy, Planning, Architecture, Media. Yun suggests that the speed of change in China dissolves all boundaries between these four pursuits.) The house sits on a lush, gently sloping hillside in view of the surrounding mountains. The architect acknowledged the house's setting between a river and the nearby mountains by cladding most of the exterior

walls in both smooth, water-polished stones and rough stones excavated from the earth. Local villagers who helped build the house spent two years collecting stones from the riverbed and carefully sorted them by color and size, according to where on the house Yun planned to install them.

The home's organization is simple and straightforward, a boxy two-story structure covering 300 square meters (3,228 square feet) and enclosed by full-story-high walls that define a series of outdoor courtyards of varying shapes and sizes. One enters between two such walls, up a short flight of stairs that overlooks a long narrow pool running the length of the home, and turns into a paved courtyard fronting the house. The courtyard elevation is dramatic: The entire two-story facade is clad in towering wood shutters that conceal glass walls and doors with dark steel frames. The shutters completely fill the space between the gridded concrete frame: when they are open, the house becomes completely permeable; when they are shut, the house takes on a hermetically sealed character.

The living spaces open onto the courtyard; behind are the kitchen, bathroom, and other services; above are bedrooms and bathrooms. Yun clad the entire interior—floors, walls, and ceilings—in plywood panels covered in woven bamboo sheeting, creating the effect of a precious wooden jewel box. The walls between the

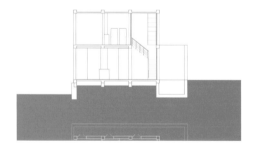

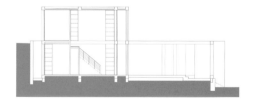

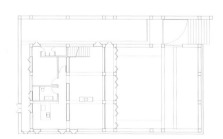

Previous spread: The main elevation overlooking the entry courtyard reveals concrete, glass, and steel, juxtaposed with walls of river stones and wooden shutters covered in woven bamboo sheathing.

Above: The boxy two-story house blends in with its rural setting in the foothills of China's Qinlin Mountain.

Left: Sections (top and center); ground-level plan (bottom).

living and service spaces conceal built-in storage. Yun
wrapped the large exterior shutters, which continue
around the perimeter of the house, in the same texture
of woven bamboo.

Yun's design has strong overtones of the work
of Louis I. Kahn, especially in his treatment of wood
panels as infill between the exposed beams and
columns of a concrete structure. And the modernist
bent is also evident in the gridded steel frames of
the floor-to-ceiling glass doors and windows, which
have a sleek, almost industrial sensibility. But the
rough bamboo surfaces and the coarse exterior walls
covered in stone give Yun's design a more rustic,
handcrafted feeling. It's these elements that anchor
the house to its mystical surroundings and keep the
building from sticking out from the landscape like a
sleekly dressed interloper. The house is timeless and
elegant, a lasting contribution to a place with a rever-
ence toward its history and natural beauty.

Opposite: A shallow reflecting pool is finished in the same rough texture of river stones used to clad the walls surrounding the courtyard.

Above left: Towering walls of glass open the airy loft-like interior to the large entry forecourt.

Above right: A narrow pool is tucked between the house and surrounding perimeter walls.

sobek house

Werner Sobek
Stuttgart, Germany 2000

Like the homes of many architects, which are often lab-
oratories for testing out theories and ideas, German
engineer Werner Sobek's own house in Stuttgart is a
live-in experiment, particularly in flexibility and energy
efficiency. The four-story glass box is a simple but
sophisticated "machine for living," to borrow a phrase
from Le Corbusier. It is a straightforward modular steel-
framed structure with complex computer controls that
maximize the already elevated environmental benefits.
And it was built in just eleven weeks.

Sited on a steep hill overlooking the city, the home
is entered on the top level via a bridge. The house
sits on the foundation of a run-down structure from the
1920s that was preserved and built upon to minimize
the cost and trouble of new excavation. Atop the existing foundation, the engineer erected a modular steel
frame stiffened by diagonal steel bracing in just four
days. In theory, the structure could also be easily dismantled for recycling or reassembly elsewhere. (Sobek
should know something about the technology: He suc-
ceeded the influential innovator of tensile fabric structures Frei Otto as head of the Institute for Lightweight
Structures and the Central Laboratory for Structural
Engineering at the University of Stuttgart.) Floor panels
of prefabricated wood span the exposed steel members; cables and vents are concealed in exposed metal
ducts running along the glass facades and fed through
the floor and ceiling plenums.

The home's pristine transparent enclosure is a
thermally efficient skin of triple glazing mounted flush
to the steel structural frame to create a smooth glass
wrapper. The air space between the outermost of
the three layers contains a metal-coated plastic foil that
reflects most of the sun's infrared radiation, which
allows light but not heat to be transmitted through the

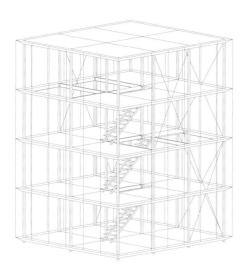
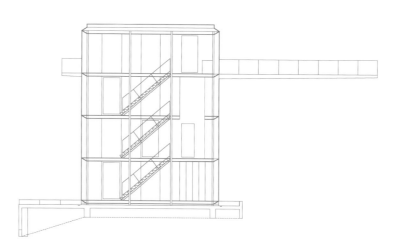

Previous spread: A bridge connects the top floor of the glass house to the top of the hillside behind it.

Above: Continuous walls of glass on all of the home's facades offer views of the surrounding landscape from every room.

Left: Axonometric of the modular structure (left), cross-section (right).

Opposite: A dramatic steel stair at the center of the house connects the disparate floor plans.

glass skin. Sobek designed an advanced heating and cooling system that takes advantage of the copious sunlight entering every inch of the facades and keeps the glass box from becoming an overheated greenhouse. Water-cooled panels in the ceilings absorb solar radiation in summer and store the collected energy; in winter, a heat transformer converts the stored solar energy into warm air that is radiated through the ceiling. There is no need for additional radiators to heat the house, which is cleanly powered by solar panels mounted to the roof. Sobek wanted to make sure the house did not produce any emissions.

Sobek spread activities throughout the four levels, using the grid of the modular structural frame— roughly 3 meters by 4 meters, or about 10 feet by 13 feet—instead of walls to imply functions within each floor. The top level contains a dining room and kitchen. Below are the main living space, bedrooms, and a workshop on the bottom floor with access to a terrace overlooking the city. An open staircase at the center of the rectangular glass box joins the disparate floor levels, offering a panoramic view as one circulates through the house. Sobek purposely kept the furnishings minimal to make the house as transparent as possible, both internally and in terms of views out from the home.

The home's "smart" technology extends to every service. Water faucets, lights, and doors and windows are linked to a central computer and activated by touchless radar sensors and voice control—so there are no light switches or door handles. A swipe of the hand opens cabinets and turns on faucets and showers, and the owner's voice opens the front door. Sobek also integrated the home's heating and cooling system into the computerized network so that, like the rest of the intelligent technical features, it can be monitored and changed by phone or computer from anywhere in the world.

Sobek's version of the machine for living has important lessons for making the home a place for energy efficiency and experimentation. As a dwelling, it has the benefits of loft-like living, with the added bonus of every space being flexible and completely open to the dramatic views of the home's surroundings. High-tech features—from the touchless controls and computerized mechanical system to the heat-reducing film in the glass walls—ensure that the house is as much an experimental work of architecture as a comfortable place to live.

Above left: Sobek left some areas of the structural frame open, to create double-height spaces.

Above right: Operable windows provide fresh air to the high-tech house.

Opposite: Structural cross-bracing and neatly arranged conduits animate the otherwise neutral glass exterior.

straw bale house

Sarah Wigglesworth Architects
London, United Kingdom 2001

The notion of building a house with bundles of straw may sound like a folly gleaned from reading "The Three Little Pigs." Yet the house that architects Sarah Wigglesworth and Jeremy Till created for themselves in a scruffy North London neighborhood is far from primitive, even though it indeed is built of straw bale walls and other offbeat materials. The experimental home also combines a facade of sandbags, a gabion structural pier, and clear polycarbonate siding in an ecologically sensitive work of architecture that involved hundreds of drawings and several years of construction to complete.

The 490-square-meter (5,272-square-foot) home and studio sits at the end of a row of Victorian cottages. The plan is an L-shape with the short leg, which houses the studio space, turning a mostly solid face to an adjacent railway line. The longer leg of the L contains the couple's living quarters. At the intersection of the two wings, a combination dining and conference room blurs the clear distinctions between work and home.

Gabions—the rock-filled metal cages developed by civil engineers as retaining walls, often seen holding back mud-slides and avalanches along roads in the Alps and other mountainous areas—support the office wing fronting the train tracks. The fact that the architects used load-bearing gabions filled with the rubble of recycled concrete walls and metal coils to absorb the rumbling vibrations of passing trains is a structural first. The exterior walls above are built up of sandbags filled with cement, sand, and lime that will also help

Previous spread: Two views of the house and office reveal the variety of materials, both traditional and unorthodox, that gives the house its unique character, including walls of stacked straw bales.

Opposite: The living spaces are wrapped primarily in glass.

Top left: Part of the office wing is clad in a quilted weatherproof fabric stretched over a wood frame.

Above right: A tree trunk slipcovering a structural column reminds visitors of the home's "green" or sustainable mandate.

Bottom left: Another part of the office structure is clad in sandbags filled with concrete to help dampen noise from an adjacent rail line.

Right: Longitudinal section (left); cross-section (right).

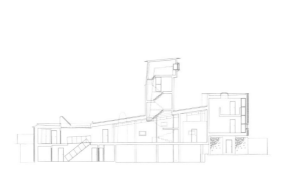

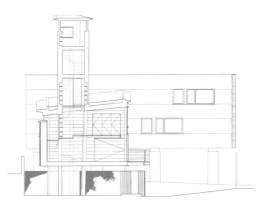

Above left: The dining area
doubles as a conference room
for the adjoining office wing.

Top right: Stairs lead from
the ground floor to the living
quarters above.

Above right: The bottom of the
tower is filled with books.

Right: First floor plan (left),
ground floor plan (right).

Opposite: A steel-framed tower
rises above the quirky compound
to create a landmark in the tough
industrial neighborhood.

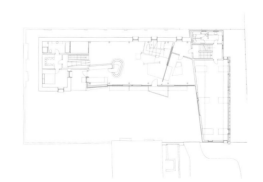

dampen noise from nearby trains. The mixture inside the plastic bags is solid, but when the bags eventually weather and decay, the rippling walls of concrete that are left will reveal the bags' woven patterns.

The remainder of the office wing is clad in a padded waterproof fabric—a simple material that has proven to last on oil rigs in the harsh climate of the North Sea—stretched over a wooden frame. The architects explain that if and when the fabric, which reminds them of a quilted duvet cover, decays, they will simply rewrap the exterior, probably in a different color fabric.

The residential wing features walls built of straw bale. The architects clearly lay out the advantages of this plentiful agricultural by-product: Straw is cheap (a few US dollars per bale), readily available, comes in standard sizes, has no embodied energy, is easy to built with, provides excellent thermal insulation, and breathes. Straw bales can be used as load-bearing walls, but Wigglesworth and Till elected to use it as infill within wood-frame walls. In this instance, the benefit is more as thick insulation on the north elevation. The architects explain that the bales must still be protected from the elements; they clad the straw walls, which they erected themselves with the help of friends at the rate of 75 square meters (805 square feet) per day, in a skin of corrugated metal and clear polycarbonate. The architects used pre-assembled steel frame for other parts of the house, including the distinctive three-story tower. Some environmental proponents tout steel as a sustainable material because it can be recycled; Wigglesworth and Till do not agree with that viewpoint. They resorted to steel because they found it the best material for the job.

The infrastructure of the home is also environmentally sensitive. Wigglesworth installed composting toilets throughout and large 3,000-gallon tanks that collect rainwater to be recycled. One tank is used to irrigate the thermally efficient planted roof; the other feeds the toilets.

With the exception of the double-duty conference and dining room, the living and working areas of the house remain distinct, with the office wing creating a barrier between the railroad tracks and the house. The entrance to the residential area is on the ground floor, up to the loft-like living area one story above. Rising through the soaring open space, with a wall of glass facing south and the solid walls of straw with three punched openings to the north, is a "tower of books." The tower, with bookcases at its base, rises up through the roof to a tiny reading room at its top. The bedroom and bath, protected by the thick straw walls, are located at the opposite end of the house.

Wigglesworth and Till's house has an unfinished look to it, and in many ways it is unfinished—or at least constantly evolving. The experiments undertaken in this highly experimental house will continue.

pedernal house

Adriana Monroy Noriega
Mexico City, Mexico 2000

In the 1950s, the Mexican modernist Francisco Artigas created a series of houses near Jardines de San Angel del Pedregal park in Mexico City, which he also designed. Artigas's houses blended International Style Modernism with local materials to give global modern style a Mexican character. One such house, the Pedernal House from the 1950s, was, relucantly, demolished by Mexico City architect Adriana Monroy Noriega in the process of building a larger two-story house on the site of the original house. (The existing single-story structure was not strong enough to support the load of an additional floor, which was necessitated by the client's requirement to double the square footage.) Monroy Noriega's renovation used the layout and the best features of the original house as a springboard for a new design that, like its predecessor, integrates a lush private garden with the house itself. In fact, a major reason that Monroy Noriega opted for demolition was that she did not want to encroach on the surrounding landscape established by Artigas's design, which she describes as captivatingly simple.

The house, now covering 720 square meters (7,747 square feet), turns a solid, imposing face to the street. The garage, a square block clad in black slate from San

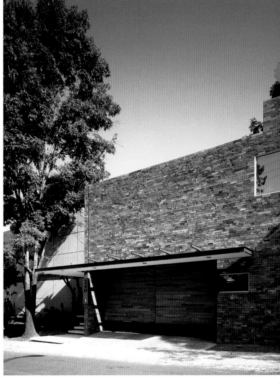

Luis Potosí in central Mexico, and a long windowless wall of concrete extending the length of the house frame the discrete front door, marked by a towering tree. Most of the foyer is taken up by a gently sloping ramp sheathed in the reddish-colored tropical hardwood *tzalam*, which leads to the upstairs bedrooms.

The main floor contains the living spaces, all of which open up to a private garden in back with sliding glass doors that extend from floor to ceiling. At one end is the large eat-in kitchen; at the other is a study and TV room for the family, with a large pivoting glass door that opens onto the garden. Separating the two is an open living/dining room with a fireplace tucked into a wall of black slate called pizarra. Behind the garage is a semidetached service wing with two additional bedrooms for the live-in staff. Upstairs are three bedrooms with a private terrace between the master suite and identical rooms for the children.

The architect's renovation features richly textured materials. The garden elevation reveals a complex interplay of natural and man-made materials: concrete, steel handrails, slate, and concrete slabs edged in rough pebbles. Inside, Monroy Noriega clad the floors in brightly polished *tzalam* wood and covered the walls in a combination of smooth and rough textures of black Mexican slate. Dramatic up- and down-lighting highlights the sophisticated play of textures.

Monroy Noriega says she was conscious of keeping a close connection between the architecture and the garden, so that the house appears to float in the landscape just as Artigas intended. On the street side, the architect laments that she had to make a more solid facade, given security concerns. While the original Artigas house was more open, current levels of protection require less openness—or more armed guards. With such exquisite materials and detailing, however, the house hardly seems like a bunker. "I am a strong believer in the natural value of materials and their essence," says Monroy Noriega. "You can get beautiful results when you respect them and use them wisely."

Previous spread: The back facade opens up to a private garden.

Above left: For security reasons, the house turns a solid concrete face to the street.

Above right: The garage block is clad in black slate from central Mexico.

Opposite: Behind the solid entry facade is a stunning skylit hallway with a ramp made of tropical hardwood leading up to bedrooms on the second floor.

CASA PEDERNAL   PEDREGAL DE SAN ANGEL
CORTE LONGITUDINAL

Opposite, top left: In the living room, a fireplace is built into a black slate wall.

Opposite, top right: Dramatic lighting along the ramp up to the second floor highlights the textures of tropical *tzalam* wood and rough slate.

Opposite, bottom: Longitudinal section (top); cross-section (bottom).

Above: At night, the rear facade becomes a glowing lantern overlooking the private garden.

neugebauer house

Richard Meier & Partners Architects
Naples, Florida, United States 1998

This 697-square-meter (7,500-square-foot) house
designed by Richard Meier in Naples, Florida, is a
striking departure from the Mediterranean Revival
architecture common throughout the region. In his signature streamlined modern style rendered in white
steel and glass, Meier created a delicate pavilion overlooking Doubloon Bay. The home's defining element
is a daring butterfly roof—a standout among homes
with red-tile roofs—that lifts up toward the bay, bringing light into the airy interior. The double-layer roof
meets local guidelines for a pitched profile, though in
a subversive manner.

In typical Meier style, the architect organized
the 1.5-acre fan-shaped site as a series of overlapping
grids, with sculptural objects standing out against
underlying geometric fields. The garage is a circular
limestone-clad drum at the entry side of the house,
adjoining a gridded grove of 25 palm trees. The house
itself is a simple rectangular bar set on a shallow
plinth paved in Spanish limestone, with a long lap pool
along the edge of the bay, which sets off the composition from the underlying field of grass.

The house is organized as a series of parallel
layers that widen from the garage toward the waterfront; every dimension is based on a strict 12-foot (3.6-
meter) module. The edge closest to the garage is a

long corridor providing access to the middle zone, a functional spine containing the kitchen, bathrooms, and other service spaces. The bedrooms and main living areas are located in the widest section, closest to the water, which is sheltered by the large butterfly roof. As the roof lifts up, it allows for narrow clerestory windows to extend the full length of the house, along both sides. Access from the foyer to the living spaces and the outdoor terrace is perpendicular to the home's primary circulation, which is parallel to the water.

One enters the house just beyond the garage, onto an elevated platform. The foyer opens frontally onto an outdoor terrace. To the right is the open living/dining area, overlooking the bay through walls of floor-to-ceiling glass. The kitchen is located behind the dining area, in the service zone running through the middle of the house. To the left of the foyer is the master suite, with a large sitting area, and, beyond another outdoor

terrace, three additional bedrooms, each with its own private bath. The farthest bedroom includes an adjoining sitting area. The architect kept the circulation to the bedrooms completely private and separate from the public spaces. To reach the rooms, one can enter either through the service corridor at the back of the house or directly from the terrace that extends the full length of the house. The rational organization allows each room to have its own access to the terrace and views of the bay while maximizing privacy.

Meier clad the landside elevation enclosing the service corridor in 2-foot-by-3-foot limestone slabs over a concrete-and-masonry frame. Narrow vertical slot windows between limestone panels and an overhead skylight extending the length of the corridor provide natural illumination. The waterfront facade is completely enclosed in a steel-framed curtain wall. The hurricane-resistant laminated glass, set in aluminum

Previous spread: Crowned by a distinctive butterfly roof, the house is a layered, linear bar structure set atop a limestone pedestal.

Above: Steps lead down from the pool deck to a lawn and the bay beyond. To the left are public living spaces; to the right are bedrooms.

Opposite: A built-in brise-soleil of thin aluminum tubes shades an open-air foyer separating the living areas from the bedroom wing.

frames, measures roughly 1 1/4 inches thick (3.2 centimeters). To keep heat and glare in check along this south- and west-facing elevation, Meier designed a system of integral sunscreens for the upper reaches of the curtain wall. One-inch-diameter (2.5-centimeter-diameter) aluminum tubes spaced 2 inches (5 centimeters) apart create a series of slender white louvers spanning between vertical supports outside the glass wall. On the overhead skylights, Meier added a ceramic frit pattern to cut down on excess light and heat gain.

Meier has designed many landmark modern houses in his nearly forty-year career. The Neugebauer House reveals the current design direction in his firm, one that incorporates more innovative structural solutions and more advanced environmental controls. Such an approach is evident in the Meier–designed new courthouse and federal building in Phoenix, Arizona, whose massive glass-enclosed atrium is naturally ventilated through a clever passive cooling system. Though the technical solutions in the Neugebauer House are not as sophisticated as in the courthouse, elements such as the integral sunscreen reveal an attention to controlling the environment, especially in the hot, sunny climate of southwest Florida.

Opposite, top: The side elevation reveals the home's layered composition, with, from left to right, an entrance to the service corridor; the kitchen and functional core; the living spaces beneath the butterfly roof; and the pool deck overlooking the water.

Opposite, bottom: A continuous skylight brings daylight into the service corridor extending the length of the house.

Above: Cross-section (top); southwest elevation (right).

Left: The open living/dining area overlooks the bay through floor-to-ceiling glass.

nenning house

Cukrowicz.Nachbaur Architekten
Hittisau, Austria 2004

The architects Andreas Cukrowicz and Anton Nachbaur-Sturm, partners in Cukrowicz.Nachbaur Architekten in Bregenz, Austria, designed a house for a carpenter and his family in Hittisau. The 320-square-meter (3,443-square-foot) Nenning House fronts the main square of this tiny hamlet with a population of just 1,879 residents, in the mountainous Vorarlberg region of Western Austria, about ten miles east of Bregenz and Lake Constance. Just a short distance away is a domed picturesque alpine church. The three-story structure, partially bermed into a hillside, contains the family's living quarters on the top two floors, as well as a duplex apartment separated from the main part of the house by a staircase. The second floor, reached by a door at the back side, away from the town square, contains the main living spaces; the third level contains bedrooms and baths. The apartment could be combined with the rest of the house to add living space for more family members. The ground floor also contains a small shop with large windows facing the town square.

Cukrowicz.Nachbaur wanted the house to reinterpret the design elements of the surrounding structures, mostly solid masonry houses with pitched tile roofs. Although the Nenning House echoes the traditional pitched profiles of its neighbors, it automatically stands apart from them because of its slatted wood exterior. (It also has reddish-colored roof tiles, just like the neighboring homes.) The mullion-less windows give the exterior a decidedly modern twist, even though their proportions are in line with the traditional windows of the existing village houses.

The exterior skin is more innovative than it might appear at first glance. On the facade facing the main street, Cukrowicz.Nachbaur designed wood shutters that slide shut to render the exterior a solid wood skin or open to reveal the simple planes of glass. On the rear facade, the architects added slatted wood shutters that flip up and onto the ceiling of narrow porches on both floors. The ground floor features a continuous porch extending the length of the living spaces; each of the three bedrooms above has its own private porch. These semi-outdoor spaces are sitting areas that allow the rooms behind them to be enclosed by glass doors and floor-to-ceiling glass walls without exposing those rooms to the cold alpine winters. Even though they are not heated, the porches create a thermal buffer zone between the glass walls and the real outside air.

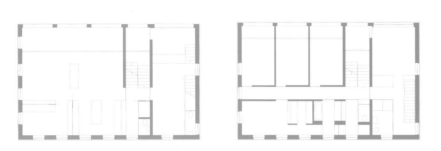

Previous spread: The house echoes the profile and tiled roof of the traditional houses surrounding it, but takes on a modern twist with slatted wood siding and mullionless windows.

Opposite, top left: Ground-floor plan (left); second-floor plan (right).

Opposite, top right: An imposing fireplace breaks the uniformity of the all-wood interior.

Opposite, bottom: Slatted shutters, which hinge up toward the roof, enclose a porch off one of the bedrooms.

Above, left: The kitchen follows a monochromatic palette, with floors, walls, ceilings, and cabinets covered in the same narrow strips of wood.

Above, right: A narrow space with windows off the ground-floor living spaces creates a year-round porch.

In pleasant weather, the family can bring out the dining table, or enjoy a quiet reading room adjoining their bedroom.

The interior is completely finished in wood: floors, walls, and ceilings. Even the kitchen cabinets are covered in the same thin strips of wood, creating a seamless interior reminiscent of a giant piece of furniture, or perhaps an enormous sauna, minus the heat. Even the kitchen table matches the pale hues of the wood floors, walls, and ceilings. Overall, the detailing is minimal, almost spare, with bare light bulbs hanging above the bedrooms.

Like Cukrowicz.Nachbaur's previous projects, the Nenning House is modest but exciting, a simple box-like structure built with great precision. The architects say their design was not meant to be flashy; rather, they wanted the structure to blend into its surrounding inconspicuously. But they wanted passersby to give the house second glance. Indeed, the Nenning House deserves a second look: It's deceptively simple, and hardly traditional.

zerlauth house

ArchitekturBüro D. I. Hermann Kaufmann
Frastanz, Austria   2003

Austrian architect Hermann Kaufmann designed a simple but striking house for clients Markus and Elisa Zerlauth in Frastanz, in the Vorarlberg region of Western Austria. Like many architects practicing in Vorarlberg, Kaufmann, whose firm is headquartered in Schwarzach, near Bregenz, is partial to designing crisp structures that reconcile hard-edged Modernism with the building traditions of this Alpine region—especially timber construction. His buildings' low-slung profiles strike a balance with the dramatic Alpine landscape.

The Zerlauth House is located on the outskirts of the small town of Frastanz, which Kaufmann describes as filled with a heterogeneous fabric of undistinguished single-family houses. The property slopes gently toward the west and distant views of the Swiss Alps. The two-story structure is buried into the hillside so that the second level opens onto a flat green lawn.

The second story contains the main living spaces, which open onto the south-facing garden through large sliding glass doors. Kaufmann considers the garden an extension of the interior living spaces, an introverted outdoor living room bounded by a swimming pool and pale concrete walls. The partially bermed lower level contains bedrooms, with large windows on the side elevations. The bedroom level creates a solid concrete base to the upstairs, an open, loft-like space with large expanses of floor-to-ceiling glass. Kaufmann visually joined the upper and lower levels with a strong, simple

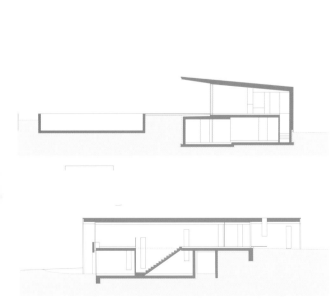

Previous spread: The wood-covered roof and glass walls of the rear facade, overlooking a pool and private garden, give a California modern feeling to this house in western Austria.

Above: The garden facade features a long band of clerestory windows above large sliding glass doors.

Left: Cross-section (top); longitudinal section (bottom).

Right: On the east facade, the folded metal wall shelters a carport.

Opposite: On the west facade, a wall of standing-seam metal folds over to create an angled roof over the living room and ground-floor bedrooms.

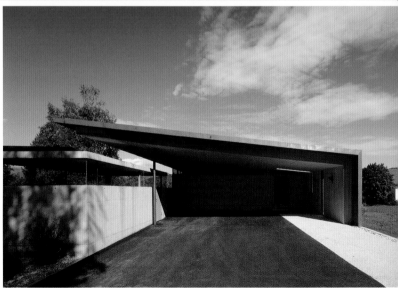

Top left: Irregularly spaced vertical windows animate the metal-clad north facade.

Above left: Concrete retaining walls define the garden and pool off the upper level of the house.

Above right: A wood deck extends the length of the south-facing garden facade, shaded by the deep roof overhang.

Right: Site plan.

Opposite, left: Dark hardwood floors contrast with lighter-colored fir covering the walls and ceilings.

Opposite, right: Walls of glass connect the open living-dining room to views of the alpine landscape.

gesture: a large copper plane that wraps the entire house. The metal wrapper creates a roof with deep overhangs above the second floor, especially over the wooden deck extending the length of the mostly glazed south elevation. On the shorter eastern end of the long rectangular house, the folded copper canopy shelters a carport. As the copper plane bends vertically, it becomes the exterior wall of the north facade, with a few vertical windows marching across the metal wall in an irregular rhythm.

The Zerlauth House is surprisingly open and casual. The connection between house and garden with huge glass doors is not typical of the closed, cellular houses of the Alps. There is an almost California-modern feeling to the design, especially the garden elevation. The West Coast sensibility continues inside, with dark hardwood floors and lighter fir covering the walls and ceilings. The upstairs interior is a breezy, casual loft, with undivided spaces that all open up to the view.

Kaufmann made sure the house was protected against the Austrian winter: He added double glazing on the garden elevation and plenty of thick wall insulation to minimize energy consumption despite the large expanses of glass. He also installed an energy-efficient heat-recovery ventilation system and solar collectors that heat water for household use. In winter, of course, so much south-facing glass makes for a warmer, brighter interior.

The California feeling ends when one views the house against the distinctive and dramatic landscape of the Austrian Alps. The home's long, linear profile works well as a base for the dramatic mountains surrounding the site, and its exterior palette of wood and dark, rich metal echo the colors of the landscape. Kaufmann's design captures the strong but sensitive architecture that characterizes the new modern design of the Vorarlberg region.

chicago house

Tadao Ando Architect & Associates
Chicago, Illinois, United States 1997

Before he built his first major commissions in the United States, Tadao Ando, the Japanese minimalist master of sublime concrete structures, designed a private house on a 75-foot-wide (23-meter-wide) site in Chicago's Lincoln Park neighborhood. The house, which Ando began to design in 1992, has the same sophisticated serenity as his Pulitzer Foundation for the Arts in St. Louis (2001) and the Modern Art Museum of Fort Worth (2002), achieved through his signature use of concrete water features.

Covering 520 square meters (5,600 square feet), the two-story concrete house is composed of two wings joined on the ground floor by a vast open living/dining room and upstairs by an outdoor terrace reached either by indoor stairs or by an exterior ramp outside the living room. The concrete ramp rises out of a shallow reflecting pool—a favorite motif in Ando's work—separating the two wings of the house. More than just a circulation element, the ramp is a meditative platform one can ascend slowly to contemplate the coolness and serenity of the outdoor water court. A spare concrete frame,

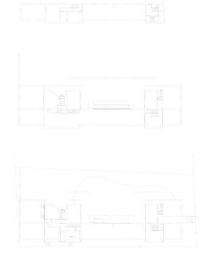

one of a series of parallel walls that define spaces within and outside of the house, spans the free-form edge of the pool farthest from the house.

One leaves the city behind and passes into an open-air court before entering Ando's sacred realm. The double-height foyer opens onto the long living/dining room, which is defined by a solid plane of concrete on one side and a wall of towering glass on the other, overlooking the gravel-bottomed reflecting pool. The ramp up to the second floor zigzags gently past the glass wall, animating the cool gallery-like space with the building's only non-orthogonal lines. Sunlight reflecting off the water creates a pattern of subtle highlights on the ceiling, while the shadow lines of the thick window mullions and the diagonals cast by the ramp just outside produce a bold graphic pattern on the living/dining room floor. In winter, when the pool is drained, the swath of bare gravel creates an abstract focal point not unlike a Japanese Zen garden.

At the opposite end of the living/dining space are the more functional, less ceremonial areas of the house: the kitchen, sitting room, library, a bedroom, and garage. There is also a small garden. Above this wing are a pair of bedrooms on the second floor and

Previous spread: A view of the rear of the house reveals its layered organization, with exterior ramps floating above a reflecting pool.

Above left: The curved concrete form at one end of the second-floor roof deck conceals a staircase.

Above, top right: The view from the sitting room extends toward a guest room across the pool.

Above, bottom right: Floor-to-ceiling glass in the loft-like living/dining area overlooks the reflecting pool and outdoor ramp.

Right: Floor plans.

Opposite, top: A large concrete span above the pool frames the composition of the rear facade.

Opposite, bottom: Sketch of rear facade with ramp.

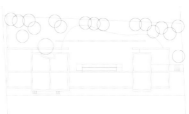

Left: Longitudinal section.

Below left: An open-air terrace on the second floor provides access to a guest room. At the opposite end is the master room, accessible from a staircase inside.

Below right: A double-height entry hall opens to views of the courtyard marking the entrance to the house.

Opposite: The concrete portal spanning the reflecting pool defines the home's outermost boundary.

the master suite on the third floor; at the other end of the house is a secluded second-floor guest room.

The palette is dominated by the architect's signature material: poured-in-place concrete. Exposed tie-holes give the rectangular concrete panels a sense of scale and pattern. While the house is an exercise in the skillful use of concrete for poetic effect, the concrete's coolness and neutral character play a secondary role to Ando's manipulation of space and natural light as tangible elements.

Although Ando may be best known for building museums, galleries, and churches, he captured the same calm, contemplative atmosphere of institutional projects in this private house. At first blush, the house might seem large and impersonal, better suited to displaying art than to living. But it soon becomes clear that the architect designed a fully functional and very private home with an added layer of atmosphere and spatial sophistication. Ando created a soothing sanctuary of space and light in a dense urban neighborhood, a refuge from the world outside.

ponce house

Mathias Klotz
Buenos Aires, Argentina 2003

The Chilean architect Mathias Klotz is one of the leading practitioners of Modernism in the Southern Cone.
With projects from university buildings to wineries
to private houses, Klotz's exquisite architecture ranges
from a regionally inflected, timber-clad style to hard-
edged glass and steel buildings as sophisticated and
well crafted as any in Europe. His work is crisp and
exciting, perhaps even more exciting because it is so
geographically distant from the dominant cultural axis
joining Asia, North America, and Europe.

One of his most recent works is the Ponce House
in San Isidro, a 1940s neighborhood in Buenos Aires.
The site is a long, narrow 2,000-square-meter (21,528-
square-foot) property overlooking the Rio de La Plata,
the wide, mighty river that defines the eastern edge of
the Argentine capital and separates Argentina from
Uruguay. The site slopes down from street level toward
the river, with tall trees defining its long sides. Klotz
did not want the house to divide the site into halves,
with a distinct front and back yard or garden; he
wanted the whole site to stay open to views of the river.

One enters the 572-square-meter (6,154-square-
foot) house at street level through a narrow portal
framed in concrete. Beyond a steel gate painted bright
red, the entry path becomes a narrow bridge as the
ground beneath begins to slope downward. A sliver of
the Rio de La Plata, with its distinctive golden-brown
color that locals liken to a lion's mane, is visible on the
horizon as one walks toward the house, framed by the
large, spare volume of the house and a dense wall of
trees to the left. Continuing along this dramatic open-
air corridor, the walkway ends in a large pool deck
overlooking the river. The deck itself an enormous concrete platform cantilevered over the steeply sloping
hillside, confirmed by the view of the back elevation
from downhill. Klotz created the suggestion of invisible
walls defining an outdoor room with a steel frame out-
lining the perimeter of the outdoor deck. (One side of
the terrace is actually enclosed by large panes of glass

within the steel frame that visually continues one of the facades of the house.)

The house itself appears to defy structural logic: A solid concrete bar floats on a glass base, which in turn floats over a solid service core. The ground floor, which contains the main living spaces, kitchen, terraces, and pool, is contained in a transparent glass volume. Glass walls in every direction open the loft-like interior to views of the dense landscape and the river in the distance. The upper level, which contains the bedrooms, is a much more solid volume cantilevered from the solid core. The upstairs level has strategically placed windows that pop out from the concrete skin and a wall of sliding glass doors that opens onto a roof deck above the ground-floor living spaces. Round porthole-shaped skylights cut into the roof bring daylight to the living areas below while animating the surface of the deck above.

From the outside, the Ponce House is a daring, dynamic piece of architecture. Inside, the architecture feels secondary to the surroundings, as the views become more important than the structure. Klotz has again created a sophisticated work that offers unexpected views and dramatic details.

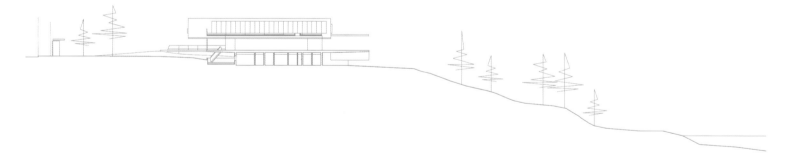

Previous spread: The entry facade is a dramatic composition, with the concrete box containing bedrooms cantilevered from the glass-enclosed ground floor. A bridge leads from the entry gate to the front door, beneath the concrete cantilever.

Opposite, top left: The entry bridge to the house is visible through a glass wall enclosing the dining area.

Opposite, top right: Stairs lead to the living spaces.

Opposite, bottom right: A glass-enclosed shower offers views outside.

Top: A steel frame hovering above the pool deck suggests the walls and ceiling of an outdoor room. In the distance is Argentina's most important river, the Rio de La Plata.

Above: Longitudinal section through site.

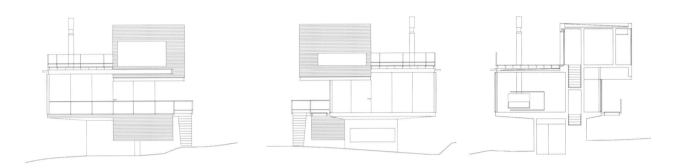

Left: Sections through
the house.

Below: The loft-like living area
flows seamlessly onto the pool
deck through a glass wall with
thin frames.

Opposite: A dusk view of
the house from the entry bridge
reveals the visually delicate
balancing act of concrete floating
over glass.

project credits

Fletcher-Page House
Kangaroo Valley, Australia 2000
Architect: Glenn Murcutt
176a Raglan St, Mosman 2088, Australia
Design Team: Glenn Murcutt and Associates,
assisted by Nick Sissons
Client: Fletcher Page
Engineer: James Taylor
Contractor: Jim Anderson (Boardwalk)

Weiss House
Cabo San Lucas, Mexico 1999–2002
Architect: Steven Harris Architects
50 Warren Street, New York, New York 10007, USA
Design Team: Tom Zook, Antonio Zaninovik, Lucien Rees Roberts
Client: George and Claire Weiss
Landscape Architect: Margie Ruddick
Contractor: Alejandro Trevino Angulo

Carter Tucker House
Victoria, Australia 1998–2000
Architect: Sean Godsell
Sean Godsell Architects, 45 Flinders Lane, Melbourne,
Victoria 3000 Australia
Design Team: Hayley Franklin, Marcus Wee
Client: Earl Carter, Wanda Tucker
Landscape Architect: Sean Godsell
Engineers: John Mullen and partners
Contractor: Kane Constructions Ltd.

De Blas House
Sevilla La Nueva, Madrid, Spain 1999–2000
Architect: Alberto Campo Baeza
Almirante 9, 28004 Madrid, Spain
Design Team: Alberto Campo Baeza, Raul Del Valle
Client: Francisco De Blas
Engineer: M. Concepcion Perez Gutierrez
Contractors: Juan Sainz

Weathering Steel House
Toronto, Canada 2002
Architect: Shim-Sutcliffe Architects
441 Queen Street East, Toronto, Ontario, Canada M5A 1T5
Design Team: Brigitte Shim, Howard Sutcliffe
Landscape Architect: Neil Turnbull
Engineers: Structural: Blackwell Engineering
Mechanical: Dr. Ted Kesik
Contractor: Kamrus Construction – Derek Nicholson
Other: Weathering Steel cladding: Tremonte Manufacturing Ltd.
Reflecting Pool: Waterarchitecture Inc.
Audio, Security, Lighting: Synergy
Interiors: Kelly Buffey

Tubac House
Tubac, Arizona, USA 1998–2000
Architect: Rick Joy Architects
400 South Rubio, Tucson, Arizona 85701, USA
Design Team: Rick Joy, Andy Tinucci, Chelsea Grassinger,
Franz Buhler
Landscape Architect: Michael Boucher Landscape Architects
Engineers: Southwest Structural Engineers, Otterbein Mechanical
Engineering Contractor: Rick Joy Architects

Vejby Strand Summer House
Vejby Strand, Denmark 1999–2000
Architect: Henning Larsens Tegnestue
Vesterbrogade 76, DK-1620, Copenhagen V, Denmark
Design Team: Henning Larsen, Peer Teglgaard Jeppesen,
Anders Park, Claus Simonsen

Client: Michael Andersen
Landscape Architect: Henrik Andersen
Engineer: Anders Christensen
Contractor: Langelinie Byg ApS / Jan Hansen

Koehler House
New Brunswick, Canada 2001
Architect: Julie Snow Architects, Inc.
527 Marquette Avenue, 2400 Rand Tower,
Minneapolis Minnesota 55402, USA
Design Team: Julie Snow, Ben Awes, Jim Larson, Connie Lindor,
Kenwood McQuade, Lucas Alm
Client: Mar Beth and David Koehler
Engineers: Cambell Comeau Engineering
Structural: John Johnson
Mechanical: Jack Snow
Contractor: Erb Builders

Casa Equis
Cañete, Peru 2002–2003
Architect: Barclay & Crousse Architecture
7 passage Saint Bernard, 75011 Paris, France
Design Team: Sandra Barclay, Jean Pierre Crousse
Engineers: Llanos y Flores Ingenieros
Contractor: Edward Barclay

Mountain Tree House
Dillard, Georgia, USA 1998–2001
Architect: Mack Scogin Merrill Elam Architects
75 JW Dobbs Avenue, Atlanta, Georgia 30303, USA
Design Team: Mack Scogin, Merrill Elam, David Yocum,
Penn Ruderman, Denise Dumais
Landscape Architect: Marchant Martin
Engineers: Structural Engineer: Palmer Engineering
Contractor: Winfred McKay Construction
Other: Lighting Designer: Ramón Noya, Ramón Luminance Design

Picture Window House
Izu, Shizuoka, Japan
Architect: Shigeru Ban Architects
5-2-4 Matsubara, Setagaya-ku, Tokyo 156-0043
Design Team: Shigeru Ban, Mamiko Ishida, Kentaro Ishida
Engineers: Structural: Hoshino Architect & Engineer
Mechanical: Chiku Engineering Consultants
Contractor: Obayashi Corporation

Zigzag House
Wollombi, New South Wales, Australia 2000
Architect: Drew Heath
Design Team: Drew Heath
Client: Cardoso/Harley
Contractor: Drew Heath

Alonso-Planas House
Barcelona, Spain 1994–1998
Architect: Carlos Ferrater & Joan Guibernau
c/ Balmes 145, 08008 Barcelona, Spain
Design Team: Carlos Ferrater Studio
Client: Alonso-Planas
Engineer: Gerardo Rodriguez
Contractor: Constructora Preufet

T House
Setagaya-ku, Tokyo, Japan 1997–1999
Architect: Toyo Ito & Associates, Architects
1-19-4 Shibuya, Shibuya-ku, Tokyo 150-0002, Japan
Engineers: Structural: Structural Design Office Oak Inc.
Mechanical: Kawaguchi Engineering Consultant Co., Ltd.
and Yamazaki Engineering Consultant Co., Ltd.
Contractor: Tokyo Tekkin Concrete Co., Ltd.

C House
Arakawa-ku, Tokyo, Japan 1999–2001
Architect: Kei'ichi IRIE + Power Unit Studio
12-1-2107 Sarugaku-cho, Sibuya-ku Tokyo 150-0033, Japan
Design Team: Power Unit Studio / Kei'ichi IRIE,
Masato UEDA
Landscape Architect: Kei'ichi IRIE + Power Unit Studio
Engineers: Structural: mias/ Masahiro Ikeda , Kenji Nawa
Contractor: Matsumoto Corporation
Other: Produce: Architecture Produce Association

Dirty House
East End, London, England 2002
Architect: David Adjaye / Adjaye Associates Ltd.
23-28 Penn Street, London N1 SDL, United Kingdom
Design Team: Josh Carver
Client: Tim Noble and Sue Webster
Engineer: Megan Yates – Techniker Ltd.
Contractor: RJ Parry Ltd.

Wall House 2
Groningen, The Netherlands 2000–2001
Architect: John Q. Hejduk (deceased)
The Estate of John Hejduk, c/o Prof. Renata Hejduk,
Arizona State University, School of Architecture,
PO Box 1605, Tempe, Arizona 85287, USA
Design Team: John Hejduk, Thomas Müller, Derk Flikkema
Client: 1974: Ed Bye, Landscape Architect, (never built)
2000–2001: The City of Groningen, The Netherlands
Landscape Architect: Ed Bye
Engineer: Ingenieursbureau Dijkhuis
Contractors: BAM Woningbouw, Nico Kool, Thermac, Zonderman,
Harryvan Slochteren, Bribus Keukens Vroomshoop, Koninklijke Mosa,
Sphinx Sanitair, Chubb Lips

Small House
Tokyo, Japan 2000
Architect: Kazuyo Sejima & Associates
7-A, 2-2-35 Higashi-Shinagawa, Shinagawa-Ku,
Tokyo 140-0002, Japan
Design Team: Kazuyo Sejima, Yoshitaka Tanase, Shoko Fukuya
Engineer: Structural: Sasaki Structural Consultants

Private House
Pride's Crossing, Massachusetts, USA 1994–1996, 1998–2000
Architect: Will Bruder Architects
111 West Monroe, Suite 444, Phoenix, Arizona 85003, USA
Design Team: Will Bruder, Ben Nesbeitt, Jack DeBartelow III,
Michael Crooks, Rob Gasparde, Duane Smyth, Joe Herzog
Client: Withheld
Landscape Architect: Michael Boucher
Engineers: Structural: Rudow & Berry, Inc. – Mark Rudow
Mechanical: Otterbine Engineering – Roy Otterbine; Reid Mechanical
Design Build
Other: CA Energy Design – Charles Avery,
Electrical: Transportex (color and textile collaboration)
Contractor: Thoughtforms Corporation – Jim Williams,
Charles Barry, Brian Norris

Compound
Casey Key, Florida, USA 2002
Architect: Toshiko Mori
180 Varick Street Suite 1322, New York, New York 10014, USA
Design Team: Toshiko Mori, TMA, *Principal Architect*; Pedro Reis,
Mary Springer, Dwayne Oyler, *Project Architects*
Client: Mike and Renee Silverstein
Landscape Architect: Toshiko Mori Architect, Ward Reasoner &
Sons – Alan "Ward" Reasoner
Engineer: Stirling & Wilbur – Steven Wilbur
Contractor: Michael Walker & Associates, Inc – Michael Walker
Other: Lighting: Tanteri & Associates – Matthew Tanteri

Fiber Optic Lighting: SGF Associates – Shozo Toyohisa
Skylights and Glass Sculpture: James Carpenter Design
Associates, Inc – James Carpenter
Daylighting Studies: Carpenter Norris Consulting – Davidson Norris

Suitcase House
Badaling Shuiguan, Beijing, China 2000–2003
Architect: EDGE Design Institute Ltd.
Suite 1604, Eastern Harbour Centre, 28 Hoi Chak Street,
Quarry Bay, Hong Kong
Design Team: Gary Chang, *Design Director*, Andrew Holt, *Chief
Designer*, Howard Chang, *Designer*, Popeye Tsang, *Designer*,
Yee Lee, *Designer*
Client: SOHO China Ltd.
Landscape Architect: Mr. Ai Wei Wei
Engineers: Structural Engineer: Qin Min-De
Contractors: China Construction 1st Division, 4th Company, The 3rd
Housing Architecture Construction Company

Flatz House
Schaan, Liechtenstein, Austria 2000
Architect: B&E Baumschlager-Eberle Architects
Lindauer Str. 31, A-6911 Lochau, Austria
Design Team: Eckehard Loidolt, Paul Martin, Marlies Sofia,
Christian Tabernigg
Client: Dr. Dietmar Flatz
Landscape Architect: Vogt Landschaftsarchitekten, Zurich
Engineers:Mechanical: GMI Gasser & Messner Ingenieure, Dornbirn (A)
Structural: Ferdy Kaiser, Mauren

Bamboo Wall House
The Great Wall at Shui Guan, Beijing, China
Architect: Kengo Kuma & Associates
3-24-8 Minami-Aoyama, Minato-ku, Tokyo
Design Team: Kengo Kuma, Kenji Miyahara, Yoshikazu Takahashi,
Budi Pradono, Teppei Ishibashi, Shigeyoshi Sugai, Katinka Temme
Client: SOHO China
Engineers: Structural: K. Nakata & Associates
Facilities: Beijing Third Dwelling Architectural Engineering Company
Contractor: Beijing Third Dwelling Architectural
Engineering Company

F2 House
Condado de Sayavedra, Estado de Mexico, Mexico 2001
Architect: Miquel Adrià, Isaac Broid & Michel Rojkind
Chicago #27 P.B., Colonia Napoles, CP 03810, Mexico
Design Team: Andrés Altesor, Agustín Pereyra, Benjamin Campos,
Hernán Cuadra, Nadia Pacheco, Paulina Goycolea
Client: Alfredo Fuentes
Engineers: Salvador Mandujano, Arturo Guerra
Contractor: Proyectos Alpha

Father's House On Jade Mountain
Lantian, Xian, China 1992–2003
Architect: MADA s.p.a.m.
Room A, 11th Floor, No.758 Nanjing West Road, Shanghai, China
Design Team: Qingyun Ma, Weihang Chen, Peter Knutson, Satoko
Saeki, Yinghui Wang, James Macgill
Client: Peijie Ma
Landscape Architect: MADA s.p.a.m.
Engineer: MADA s.p.a.m.
Contractors: Exterior: Zongqi Fan
Interior: Shanghai Dumiao Interior Decoration Co., Ltd.
Other: All residents of Lantian who helped with collecting and
transporting the stones

Sobek House
Stuttgart, Germany 1999–2000
Architect: Werner Sobek
Albstr. 14, 70597 Stuttgart, Germany
Client: Ursula and Werner Sobek

Landscape Architect: Werner Sobek
Engineers: Structural: Werner Sobek Ingenieure
Climate: Transsolar
Contractor: SE Stahltechnik

Straw Bale House
North London, England 1997–2001
Architect: Sarah Wigglesworth Architects
10 Stock Orchard Street, London N7 9RW, United Kingdom
Design Team: Sarah Wigglesworth, Jeremy Till, Gillian Horn,
Michael Richards
Client: Sarah Wigglesworth and Jeremy Till,
Sarah Wigglesworth Architects
Landscape Architect:
Engineer: Price & Myers
Contractors: Koya Construction Ltd
Other: Designer's Team and Collaborators: Gillian Horn &
Michael Richards

Pedernal House
Pedregal de San Angel, Mexico City, Mexico 1999–2000
Architect: Adriana Monroy Noriega
Cañada 216, Jardines del Pedregal, México D.F. 01900.
Design Team: Adriana Monroy Noriega
Client: Sandoval-Monroy Familiy
Landscape Architect: Adriana Monroy Noriega
Engineer(s): Altec Ingenieria
Contractors: Altec Ingenieria
Other: Aluminum: Alcrisarq SA de CV
Kitchen: Piacere
Onix: Sordo-Noriega
Slate: Enzo Giustti Marble

Neugebauer House
Naples, Florida, USA 1995–1998
Architect: Richard Meier & Partners
475 10th Ave, 6th Floor, New York, New York 10018, USA
Design Team: Richard Meier, Thomas Phifer
Client: Klaus Neugebauer
Engineers: Structural and Mechanical Engineers: Ove Arup & Partners
Contractors: Newbury North Associates
Other: Curtain Wall Consultant: R.A. Heintges
Lighting Consultant: Fisher Marantz Stone

Nenning House
Hittisau, Austria
Architect: cukrowicz.nachbaur architects
Anton-Schneider-Strasse 4a, A 6900 Bregenz, Austria
Design Team: Andreas Cukrowicz, Anton Nachbaur-Sturm,
Christian Moosbrugger, Saskia Jaeger
Client: Brigitte and Hermann Nenning
Landscape Architect: Markus Cukrowicz
Engineer: Armin Bischof
Contractor: Zimmerei Nenning Hittisau

Zerlauth House
Frastanz, Austria
Architect: Hermann Kaufmann
Sportplatzweg 5, A-6858 Schwarzach
Design Team: Mrs. DI Juliane Wiljotti, Mr. BM Ing. Norbert Kaufmann
Client: Mr. Markus and Mrs. Elisa Zerlauth
Engineers: Structural: M+G Ingenieure, Feldkirch
Electrical: Manuel Krekeler, Rankweil
Plumbing, heating, ventilation: Reinhard Moser, Satteins

Chicago House
Chicago, Illinois, USA 1992–1997
Architect: Tadao Ando & Associates
5-23 Toyosaki 2-Chome Kita-ku, Osaka 531-0072, Japan
Design Team: Tadao Ando, Masataka Yano
Engineers: Structural: Cohen Barreto Marchertas, Inc.,

Electrical: Dickerson Engineering, Inc.
Mechanical: Brian Berg & Associates, Ltd.
Contractor: Zera Construction
Other: Photographer: Shigeo Ogawa

Ponce House
Buenos Aires, Argentina 2000–2003
Architect: Mathias Klotz
Los Colonos 0411, Providencia, Santiago, Chile
Design Team: Mathias Klotz, Pablo Riquelme
Client: Hernan Ponce
Landscape Architect: Juan Grimm
Engineer: Enzo Valladares
Contractor: Stieglitz
Other: Technical Inspection: SEWECO

further reading

The following selection of titles are divided into three sections: books on building design and construction; theoretical books on society and culture; books on and by the architects featured in this volume.

Design and Construction

Arieff, Allison and Bryan Burkhart. *Prefab* (Salt Lake City: Gibbs, Smith, 2002).

Cerver, Francisco Asensio. *House Details* (Arco Editorial Team, Plans of Architecture series, 1997).

Frampton, Kenneth. *Studies in Tectonic Culture: the Poetics of Construction in Nineteenth and Twentieth Century Architecture* (Cambridge, MA: MIT Press/Graham Foundation, 1998).

Daguerre, Mercedes. *20 Houses by 20 Architects*. (Milan: Electa Architecture, 2005)

Friedman, Alice T. *Women and the Making of the Modern House* (New York: Harry N. Abrams, 1998).

Gollings, John and Michell, George. *New Australia Style* (Australia: Thames and Hudson, 1999).

Herbert, Gilbert. *The Dream of the Factory Made House* (Cambridge, MA: MIT Press, 1984).

Melhuish, Clare (ed) *Architecture and Anthropology*, AD Profile 124 (London Academy Editions, 1996).

Melhuish, Clare. *Modern House 2* (London: Phaidon Press, 2000).

Oliver, Paul. *Dwellings the House across the World* (London: Phaidon Press, 1987).

Phaidon Press (ed). *The Phaidon Atlas of Contemporary World Architecture* (London: Phaidon Press, 2004).

Phaidon Press (ed). *The Phaidon Atlas of Contemporary World Architecture Travel Edition* (London: Phaidon Press, 2005).

Phaidon Press (ed). *10 x 10* (London: Phaidon Press, 2000).

Phaidon Press (ed). *10 x 10 _ 2.* (London: Phaidon Press, 2005).

Pollock, Naomi. *Modern Japanese House* (London: Phaidon Press, 2005).

Rapoport, Amos. *House Form and Culture* (New Jersey: Prentice Hall, 1969).

Russell, Barry. *Building Systems, Industrialization and Architecture* (John Wiley and Sons, 1981).

Spiller, Neil. *Digital Dreams, Architecture and the New Alchemic Technologies* (London: Ellipsis, 1998).

Riley, Terrence. *The Un-private House* (New York: Museum of Modern Art, 1999).

Ryan, Deborah S.. *The Ideal Home through the Twentieth Century* (London: Hagar Publishing, 1997).

Sudjic, Deyan. *Home: the Twentieth Century House.* (London: Laurence King, 1999).

Venturi, Robert. *Complexity and Contradiction in Architecture.* (New York: Museum of Modern Art, 1966).

Waterson, Roxana. *The Living House* (Oxford: Oxford University Press, 1991).

Welsh, John. *Modern House* (London: Phaidon Press, 1995).

Society and Culture

Bachelard, Gaston. *The Poetics of Space* (Boston: Beacon Press, 1969). Originally published in French, 1958.

Bourdieu, Pierre. *Outline of a Theory of Practice* (Cambridge; CUP, 1977); and Distinction: A Social Critique of the Judgment of Taste (London: Routeledge, 1984).

Buchli, Victor. *An Archaeology of Socialism* (Oxford: Berg Publishers, 1999).

Carsten, Janet and Hugh-Jones, Stephen. *About the House* (Cambridge, MA: CUP, 1995).

Chapman, Tony and Hockey, Jenny (eds). *Ideal Homes?: Social Change and Domestic Life* (London: Routeledge, 1999). See essay by Tim Brindley, "The Modern House in England."

Colomina, Beatriz. *Privacy and Publicity* (Cambridge, MA: MIT Press, 1995).

Frampton, Kenneth. *Modern Architecture: A Critical History* (London: Thames and Hudson, 1992).

Hiddenobu, Jinnai. *Tokyo: A Spatial Anthropology* (California: University of California Press, 1995).

Kent, Susan. *Domestic Architecture and the Use of Space* (Cambridge: Cambridge University Press, 1990).

Lambert, Phyllis, ed. *Mies in America* (Montreal and New York: The Canadian Centre for Architecture, The Whitney Museum of American Art, 2001).

Lovins, Amory. *Natural Capitalism: Creating the Next Industrial Revolution* (New York: Little Brown & Company, 1999).

Mackay, H (ed). *Consumption and Everyday Life* (London: Sage, 1997).

Mernissi, Fatima. *Beyond the Veil* (London: Al Saqui Books, 1995).

Mitchell, William. *City of Bits* (Cambridge, MA: MIT Press, 1995); and *E-topia* (MIT, 1999).

Miller, D. *Household as Cultural Idiom in Modernity: An Ethnographic Approach* (Oxford: Berg Publishers, 1993).

Mori, Minoru, Hiroo Yamagata, and Bruce Mau. *New Tokyo Life Style Think Zone.* (Tokyo: Mori Building Co., 2001).

Ravetz, Alison and Turkington, David. *English Domestic Environments 1914-2000* (London: E & F N Spon, 1995).

Reed, Christopher. *Not at Home: the Suppression of the Domestic in Modern Art and Architecture* (London: Thames and Hudson, 1996).

Silverstone, Roger and Hirsch, Eric (eds). *Consuming Technologies: Media and Information in Domestic Spaces* (London: Routeledge, 1992. (See essay by Sonia Livingston, "The Meaning of Domestic Technologies.")

Tilley, Christopher. *A Phenomenology of Landscape* (Oxford: Berg Publishers, 1994).

Tilley, Christopher. *Ethnography and Material Culture, from The Sage Handbook of Ethnography*, Atkinson, P, et al (eds) (London: Sage, 2000).

Virilio, Paul. *Open sky* (London: Verson, 1997).

Wilson, William Julius. "The State of American Cities," from *Social Exclusion and the Future of Cities* (CASE paper 35, London School of Economics, 2000).

Architect Monographs

Allen, Steven and Horacio Torrent (texts). *2G #26: Mathias Klotz.* (Barcelona: Gustavo Gili, 2003).

Ambasz, Emilio and Shigeru Ban. *Shigeru Ban* (New York: Princeton Architectural Press, 2001).

Arieff, Allison and Bryan Burkhart. *Prefab* (Utah: Gibbs, Smith, 2002).

Beck, Haig and Jackie Cooper. *Glenn Murcutt: A Singular Architectural Vision* (Australia: Images Publishing Group, 2002).

Bognar, Botond and Kengo Kuma. *Kengo Kuma: Selected Works* (New York: Princeton Architectural Press, 2004).

Chang, Gary et al.. *Suitcase House* (Map Book Publishers, 2004).

Curtis, William J.R. et al.. *Carlos Ferrater* (Barcelona: Actar, 2000).

Campo Baeza, Alberto and Antonio Pizza. *Alberto Campo Baeza* (California: Gingko Press, 2000).

Dal Co, Francesco. (ed) *Tadao Ando* (London: Phaidon Press 1995).

Drew, Philip. *Touch This Earth Lightly: Glenn Murcutt in His Own Words* (Australia; Duffy & Snellgrove, 1999).

El Croquis 77i/99: Sejima + Nishizawa (Madrid: El Croquis, 2001).

Frampton, Kenneth. *Modern Architecture: A Critical History* (Thames and Hudson, 1992).

Frampton, Kenneth. *Richard Meier* (Milano: Electa Architecture 2003).

Fromonot, Francoise. *Glenn Murcutt: Buildings and Projects 1962 to 2003* (second edition) (London: Thames & Hudson, 2003)

Hays, K. Michael. *Sanctuaries: The Last Works of John Hejduk* (New York: The Whitney Museum of American Art, 2003).

Ito, Toyo. *Blurring Architecture*. (Milano: Charta, 2000).

Jodidio, Philip. *Ando: Complete Works* (Bekedikt Taschen Verlag, 2004).

Joy, Rick. *Rick Joy: Desert Works* (New York: Princeton Architectural Press, 2002).

Lambert, Phyllis, ed. *Mies in America* (Montreal and New York: The Canadian Centre for Architecture, The Whitney Museum of American Art, 2001).

Maffei, Andrea. *Toyo Ito: Works, Projects, Writing* (Milano: Electa Architecture, 2002).

McQuaid, Matilda. *Shigeru Ban* (London: Phaidon Press, 2003).

Meier, Richard et al. *Richard Meier Architect Volume 4* (New York: Rizzoli International, 2004).

Morgan, Conway Lloyd. *Show Me the Future: Engineering and Design by Werner Sobek* (New York: Princeton Architectural Press, 2004).

Mori, Minoru, Hiroo Yamagata, and Bruce Mau. *New Tokyo Life Style Think Zone* (Tokyo: Mori Building Co., 2001).

Mori, Toshiko, ed. *Immaterial / Ultramaterial* (New York: George Braziller, 2002).

Mori, Toshiko. *Textile / Tectonic: Architecture, Material, and Fabrication* (New York: George Braziller, 2005).

Pare, Richard. *Tadao Ando: The Colours of Light* (London: Phaidon Press, 1996).

Pare, Richard. *Tadao Ando: The Colours of Light* (mini) (London: Phaidon Press, 2000).

Preziosi, Massimo. *Carlos Ferrater: Works and Projects* (Milano: Electa Architecture, 2002).

Riley, Terence. *The Un-Private House* (New York: The Museum of Modern Art, 1999).

Snow, Julie and Janet Abrams. *Julie Snow, Architects* (New York: Princeton Architectural Press, 2005).

Steele, James. *R.M. Schindler* (Benedikt Taschen Verlag, 1999).

Steiner, Dietmar and Lisbeth Waechter-Böhn. *Carlo Baumschlager Dietmar Eberle* (Springer-Verlag, 1996).

Van Schaik, Leon. *Sean Godsell* (Milano: Electa Architecture, 2004).

Vindum, Kjeld et al.. *Henning Larsen: The Architect's Studio* (Denmark: Louisiana Museum of Modern Art, 2002).

Wigglesworth, Sarah and Jeremy Till, eds. *The Everyday and Architecture* (London: Academy Editions, 1998).

index

photo credits

All illustrations were generously provided by the architects, unless otherwise specified. Photographic sources are listed where possible, but the publisher will endeavor to rectify any inadvertent omissions.

Phaidon Press Limited
Regent's Wharf
All Saints Street
London N1 9PA

Phaidon Press, Inc.
180 Varick Street
New York, NY 10014

www.phaidon.com

First published 2005
Reprinted in paperback 2006
© 2005 Phaidon Press Limited

ISBN 0 7148 4628 7

A CIP catalogue record for this book is available from the
British Library.

Designed by Ariel Apte and Sarah Gephart, mgmt. Design
Printed in China